ISLAND IN THE STREAM

ISLAND IN THE STREAM

A Quick Case Study of Taiwan's Complex History

APRIL C. J. LIN
&
JEROME F. KEATING

Second Edition

SMC PUBLISHING INC.
Taipei

SMC PUBLISHING INC.
P.O. Box 13-342, Taipei 106,
Taiwan, ROC
☎ (886-2) 2362-0190
Fax (886-2) 2362-3834
E-mail: weitw@smcbook.com.tw
http://www.smcbook.com.tw

ISBN 957-638-576-8

Contents

III   THE JAPANESE ERA

IV THE REPUBLIC OF CHINA

Dutch impression of
aborigines, 17th century.

Fort Santo Domingo, Tamsui.*

Photos: Jerome Keating.

Fort Provincia at sunset. (Photo: Courtesy of National Central Library, Taiwan Branch.)

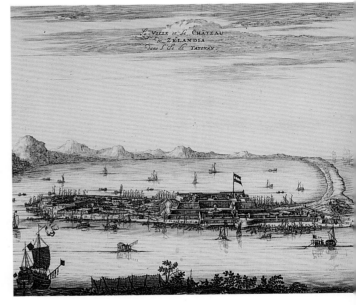

Fort Zeelandia, Dutch occupation.

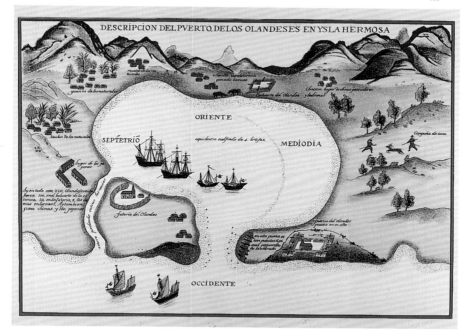

Spanish map of Dutch fortifications at Anping.

Image and seal of Shi Lang. Ch'ing Era.

Cheng Ch'eng Kung (Photo: Courtesy of National Central Library, Taiwan Branch.)

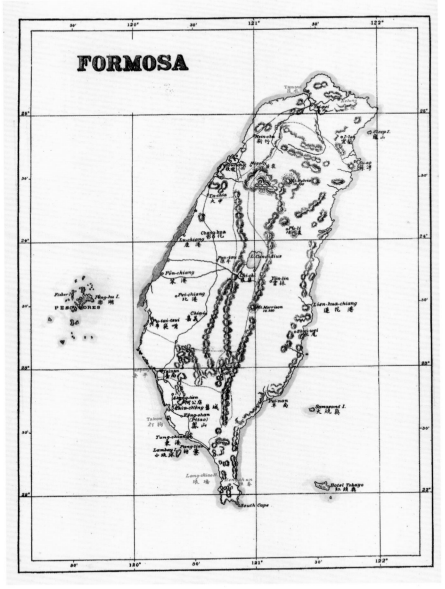

Map of Taiwan. We highlight four ports opened as a result of Tientsin Treaty (1858) and Hengchun where Japanese landed in 1874 in Peony Tribe Affair. Some other locations in this 1891 map are not geographically accurate.

THE JAPANESE EXPEDITION TO FORMOSA — GENERAL SAIGO AND THE NATIVE CHIEFS, AFTER THE LATTER HAD TENDERED THEIR SUBMISSION

The Illustrated London News, February 27, 1875.

Keelung, cemetery for French military killed in 1884-85.*

Keelung, Ch'ing Era cannon overlooks harbor; British attack repulsed in Opium War, 1841.*

Flag of Taiwan Republic, 1895.

Taiwan Republic stamp and post mark.

This Japanese landing memorial near Keelung was destroyed, but later rebuilt to symbolize resistence.

Painting illustrating Japanese troops entering Taipei city in 1895.

Taipei Station in Ch'ing Era.

Taipei Station in Japanese Era.

Traditional Sugar Cane Plant, Ch'ing Era.

Sugar Cane Factory, Japanese Era.

Japanese military exploit camphor monopoly in mountains.

Placing tea in boxes, Japanese Era.

View of the River Tamsui at Toatutia, Japanese Era.

Ami Tribe, Japanese Era.

Aborigines of the Ami Tribe in colorful dance costumes at Harvest Festival, 2000.*

The members of Xing Ming Hui, Taiwanese students studying in Japan, 1920 (Photo: Courtesy of Li Chih-Chang, *Photograph of Lin Family in Wu-Feng*, p. 128.)

Japanization of Taiwanese, 1937. (Photo: Courtesy of *A History of Taiwan's Colonial Rule*, p. 110.)

Taiwanese technicians at a Training Center to help war effort, Japanese Era.

Japanese use aborigines to fight aborigines in Mu-Sha Affair.

Japanese use aircraft to spread poison gas in Mu-Sha Affair.

Aboriginal volunteers to assist Japan in South Asia, WWII. (Photo: Courtesy of *A History of Taiwan's Colonial Rule*, p. 133.)

People welcome KMT troops in 1945; note: The National Flag is backwards.

KMT Nationalist troops evacuated to Taiwan in 1949; note: wide range of ages.

President Lee Teng-hui apologizes to the people for the 2-28 affair (February 28, 1995). (Photo: Courtesy of Academia History.)

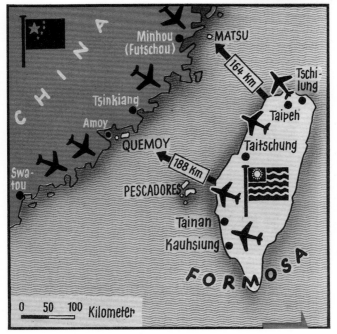

1950's rendition of PRC-ROC standoff.

President Lee Teng-hui, Taiwan's first directly elected President. (Photo: Courtesy of Government Information Office.)

Chen Shui-bian, Taiwan's second directly elected President. (Photo: Chang Chin Yuan)

Taipei: traditional style architecture, foreground; contemporary style, background.*

Chronology

1492	Columbus comes to the Americas seeking a westward way to India.
1497	Vasco da Gama sails around the Cape of Storms renaming it Cape of Good Hope. An eastern sea route is now opened to India and beyond. He reaches Macau, which will be later colonized by the Portuguese.
1500	The aborigines make up approximately 98% of the population of Taiwan.
1521	Ferdinand Magellan in an attempt to circumnavigate the globe dies in the Philippines. One of his five ships will complete this journey. The Spanish will return to colonize the Philippines.
1557	The Portuguese formally colonize Macau.
1593	Japanese king, Toyotomi Hideyoshi, sends an ambassador to the "High Mountain People" on Taiwan.
1619	The Dutch found Batavia (Jakarta) and solidify their control of Indonesia.
1624	The Ming and the Dutch fight over Penghu (the Pescadores); the Dutch occupy southwest Taiwan.

1625 | Japanese traders protest Dutch taxes in Taiwan.

1626 | The Spanish stake a claim in northwest Taiwan where they will build Fort Santo Domingo. They will be driven out in 1643.

1635 | The Japanese begin their period of isolationism and abandon any influence in Taiwan. They will not return until after Perry "opens up" Japan in 1853.

1644 | The Manchus take over China.

1662 | Cheng Ch'eng Kung (Koxinga) and the Ming loyalists retreat and drive the Dutch from Taiwan.

1683 | The Manchus take Taiwan. They maintain a passive rule over the island. Uprisings and revolts occur every three to five years.

1854 | Admiral Perry visits Taiwan and suggests the United States appropriate the island. His recommendation is ignored.

1858 | The Tientsin Treaty opens four ports on Taiwan to western trade and interest.

1871 | The "Peony Tribe Incident" reinvolves the Japanese with Taiwan.

1884 | The French briefly occupy northern Taiwan.

1885 | Taiwan becomes a Province of China.

1895 | Taiwan is ceded to Japan in the treaty of Shimonoseki. It will be their colony until 1945.

1921   The Taiwanese begin the first of many petitions for representation in the Japanese Imperial Diet.

1945   Taiwan receives representation in the Japanese Imperial Diet as World War II ends. Taiwan is placed under the protection of the Republic of China with its status to be determined.

1947   Taiwanese anger over ROC misgovernment explodes in the 2-28 incident.

1949   Martial law is imposed in Taiwan as the ROC army retreats from the mainland.

1950   The Korean War breaks out. Taiwan becomes part of the Western Bloc.

1971   The ROC loses its seat in the United Nations.

1979   The United States transfers its embassy from the ROC to the PRC.

1987   Martial law is lifted in Taiwan.

1996   In the first democratic presidential election with direct vote in Taiwan, Lee Teng-hui is re-elected president of the ROC by the people.

2000   In the second democratic presidential election Chen Shui-bian of the Democratic Progressive Party becomes the first non-KMT president in a peaceful transference of power. Aborigines make up less than 2% of Taiwan's population.

Preface

Islands can raise unique questions on national sovereignty. They have clearly defined borders that mark them as separate; yet this separateness especially when combined with small size does not automatically confer sovereignty. They are more prone to be "discovered, claimed or annexed" by other countries seeking benefit from their strategic location or resources and ignoring the resident population.

The Spratly Islands, for example, are a series of small, barely habitable islands, reefs and cays that lie in the South China Sea between Vietnam and the Philippines. For strategic purposes, France (then governing Vietnam) occupied the islands between 1933 and 1939; the Japanese had a submarine base there during World War II. In 1951, however, Japan renounced all claims to the Spratlys. Six other countries, Brunei, Malaysia, the People's Republic of China, the Philippines, the Republic of China and Vietnam, all hundreds of miles from the islands, quickly staked a claim to sovereignty over the islands. Why? The reasons were simple, strategic influence and the possibility of oil and mineral deposits.

Most of these six nations have stationed military personnel on different islands of the Spratlys to claim de facto ownership; all are searching the past to support de jure claims. Several of the nations are negotiating on how to settle claims; two nations, the People's Republic of China and Vietnam have already had a military conflict over the nearby Paracel Islands.

The Falkland Islands (some 300 miles off the southern tip of Argentina) are another example though different in history. Here Argentina and Great Britain continue to dispute sovereignty rights. Argentina bases its claim on papal bulls of 1493 and the Treaty of Tordesillas that ceded the islands to Spain. Since Argentina over-threw Spanish rule in 1816, it contends that it owns the islands. The British claim that they had settlements in the latter 1700's and have had de facto rule over the islands since 1833; they wish the sovereignty of the islands to be the result of self-determination as recognized in the United Nations charter. England and Argentina went to war over these islands in 1982 and their status is still in dispute.

Taiwan is a large island situated at the juncture of the Ryukyu Islands extending down from the islands of Japan and the Batan Islands extending up from the islands of the Philippines. In square miles, Taiwan is larger than the combined area of the states of Massachusetts and Connecticut or that of the country of Belgium. It lies 100 miles off the southeast coast of mainland China, a distance further than that of Cuba to the United States. Nevertheless, the Republic of China on Taiwan has had its own history of nations looking to utilize its position.

The population of Taiwan is larger than that of 75% of the

countries in the United Nations. Countries like Liechtenstein with little over 32,000 people or the island kingdom of Palau (Belau) with approximately 19,000 people are voting members of the UN; Taiwan with over 23,000,000 people has lost its vote. How it lost its seat in the UN is part of its complex situation, but the irony remains that Palau with only 19,000 could vote on matters concerning the 23,000,000 of Taiwan.

In economy Taiwan has consistently ranked in the top 15 among all the nations of the world. Other countries gladly trade with Taiwan and treat it as a separate country economically, culturally and most other ways. Still, they will not give it political recognition and diplomatic status. The dispute lies with the claim that the People's Republic of China makes to Taiwan, and the fact that such countries do not wish to challenge this disparity and jeopardize their opportunities with the greater China market.

What defines a nation? When new countries and nations emerge from changing borders created by world war, by colonialism and by economics, historians face this repeating question. Is it historic possession? Ethnic background? De facto might makes right? De jure agreements? What makes a nation a nation and what confers national sovereignty? Does self-determination or democracy enter into the equation?

Ryotaro Shiba (司馬遼太郎), the Japanese historical novelist, addressed this issue in his work Kaido O Yuku-Taiwan-Hen. He further ponders the question of nationhood each time he travels to Taiwan, for Taiwan more than any other place has constantly had to adapt to the problem of defining its nationhood.

At least five different flags have flown over Taiwan in the past four hundred years. With each new regime, the people on the island have had to make adaptations. Whether it be to new tax laws, languages, religions, ideologies etc., the people of the island were compelled to change their life style to fit in with each new government. These changing circumstances of having a variety of new rulers can create confusion but can also create a unique identity.

Amidst all this change, has an incoming regime ever asked the people of the island what their aspirations are? This lack of consideration is the deep, underlying meaning of what Lee Teng-hui (李登輝), the first directly elected president of Taiwan, conveyed in conversations with Mr. Shiba in 1995 as Lee spoke of the "Taiwanese Sadness."

The reality of Taiwan's ambivalent situation is still evident in its current struggles with democracy. At the end of 1945, after being a part of the Japanese Empire for fifty years, the island found itself with two distinct resident groups of people. One was the majority Taiwanese who had settled the island for more than one hundred years and aspired to self-government or at least self-representation. The other was the Kuomintang (KMT) the Chinese Nationalist government retreating from mainland China. The KMT did not exist when Japan acquired Taiwan, but had been given the island by the Allies after World War II in accord with the Cairo Declaration of 1943. At this conference in North Africa, President Roosevelt, Generalissimo Chiang Kai-shek and Prime

Minister Churchill issued the following general statement.

> The three great Allies are fighting this war to restrain and punish the aggression of Japan. They covet no gain for themselves and have no thought of territorial expansion. It is their purpose that Japan shall be stripped of all the islands in the Pacific which she has seized or occupied since the beginning of the first World War in 1914, and that all the territories Japan has stolen from the Chinese, such as Manchuria, Formosa and the Pescadores, shall be restored to the Republic of China. Japan will also be expelled from all other territories which she has taken by violence and greed. The aforesaid three great powers, mindful of the enslavement of the people of Korea, are determined that in due course Korea shall become free and independent. (Cairo Declaration.)

Fleeing the communists with whom they were losing a civil war, the KMT settled and governed the island. By 1949 the KMT numbered some two million Chinese, including soldiers, public servants and refugees. Some Taiwanese have called it their most recent invasion. The end result was that people with two different ideologies found themselves living on one island, creating a sense of "Two Republics on One Island." One could be called the Republic of Taiwan, the other the Republic of China on Taiwan.

Taiwan has seen many governments; the aborigines were the original settlers, later came the Dutch, the Spanish, the Ming Loyalists, the Ch'ing Manchus, the Japanese and the KMT.

Ironically, the People's Republic of China, a government whose flag had never flown over the island, now claims the island.

Political power on Taiwan has been transferred so frequently in the past four centuries that the people of Taiwan are to be credited with a remarkable resiliency and capability to adjust to each new set of circumstances. A proverb states, "Policy is usually made by government, counter measures always come from the people." The recent elections of March 2000 represent a different changing of the guard. The people of Taiwan directly and freely chose their leader from the opposition party. It was a peaceful transference of power and one that may mark a new era between the Taiwanese and KMT.

The following brief work hopes to show that, though Taiwan has often been a pawn and/or a political football in its past, its people have their own perspective on this diverse history. It is their feelings on this issue that explain the reason why 70% of the population supported President Lee Teng-hui's directive that all dealings with the People's Republic of China should be done on a "state to state within one country" basis.

This work will look at Taiwan and its history primarily from the sixteenth century when the European powers entered the picture and its diverse identity began to take shape. It will draw from Chinese, Japanese and Western sources.

The work can be read not only as a brief history of this controversial island, but also as a case study that presents the deeper complex questions and issues involved in nationhood and sovereignty. As such we hope it can be used as a reference, supplement or discussion source for history, political science, sociology and other courses. Probing questions will be raised at the end of each chapter to encourage further study and analysis.

At the end of each chapter, we provide a few works that interested readers can read if they wish more detailed information on the topics addressed. There is no attempt to be all-inclusive or to be evaluative on the vast amount of works available. Since our research has drawn from Chinese, English and Japanese sources we will list from all three languages. For those who read only English, we ask their indulgence.

The second edition contains an update on Chen Shui-bian's first year in office, and quotes from President Truman as regards Taiwan's status in 1950. The statements from the Coiro Conference, Potsdam Conference and the San Francisco Treaty formerly presented in an appendix have been incorporated into the text.

As regards romanization of Chinese characters, the Pin-yin system will be favored, except for instances where the Wade-Giles system (used in Taiwan) has made such usage more commonplace. Chinese characters will be placed after the first mention of names for clarification.

I

The Era of Global Navigation

Ihla Formosa: A New Name

For centuries, Taiwan had little contact or involvement with the countries surrounding it and was in total isolation from the western world. It appeared in Chinese records from the Sui Dynasty on but the mention was not one of territorial claim. Taiwan was seen as one of many islands in the Taiwan Strait and a place for potential exploration. Mainlanders fleeing the takeover of China by the Mongols (Yuan Dynasty, 1263—1368) could have retreated there but that is difficult to prove by historical records. Otherwise it had been a home for fisherman, traders, and aborigines. Its isolation, however, came to an abrupt end in the period of Global Navigation by the European powers (15th to 17th Centuries).

During that time, the maritime European powers were pushing their sea-going vessels to their limits. They pursued a course of exploration, colonization, trade linkage and religious proselytization of regions of the world hitherto unvisited. The first to enter Asian waters were the Portuguese. In 1497 Vasco da Gama had led an expedition around the Cape of Storms at the southern tip of Africa, and renamed it the Cape of Good Hope. With this name he expressed European expectations of the opening sea routes to

India. On this same expedition, da Gama also reached and landed at present day Macau. By 1511, the Portuguese were in control of trade routes between Lisbon, Goa (India) and Malacca (Malaysia). With Malacca as a trading and missionary base, the Portuguese expanded their influence into southern and eastern Asia. Their ultimate goal was to establish trade with China and Japan. They accomplished this with a route linking Macau (officially colonized in 1557) and Hirato in Japan. In the mid-1500's as one of the Portuguese ships was en route to Tanegashima, an island of southern Japan, it discovered Taiwan and gave it the name "Ihla Formosa--the beautiful island." Formosa would be the name the island would maintain in the western world until mid 20th Century. In this text we will use the names Taiwan and Formosa interchangeably.

A Pirate Base

While certainly a beautiful island, Formosa was also a pirate base. Pirates from Japan as well as China had found the island a relatively unprotected refuge as they plied their trade. The Japanese pirates had their primary bases in Kyushu and Shikoku and formed armed trading groups with Chinese and Korean members. They used Portuguese as a lingua franca in the slave trade.

These pirate groups constantly tormented the Ming Dynasty (1368—1644) and were given the name "Wokou" (倭寇) which is translated as "Japanese raiders or bandits." Formosa provided them with an excellent place for retreat, fresh water and supplies after they had attacked Ming vessels and coastal cities. The farthest place the government officials of the Ming pursued these pirates was the Penghu Archipelago (the Pescadores) in the Taiwan Strait. Because of the pirates, the Ming had severely restricted travel and trade abroad.

An Aboriginal Nation?

Long before the presence of the international pirate groups, numerous aboriginal tribes were already present on the island. The aborigines were of two types, the mountain people and the plains people. In the mountains were the Atayal, Saisiyat, Tsou, Bunun, Rukai, Paiwan, Ami, Puyuma and Yami, now considered the nine major tribes of Taiwan. On the plains were numerous Pingpu groups but these would eventually become extinct through inter-marriage and assimilation with the Chinese.

In looking for their origins, many theories abound. Some consider that the aborigines are of Malay-Polynesian stock and had migrated from the south when lower ocean levels allowed land connections between Indonesia, the Philippines and Taiwan. Other theories have linked them with the Japanese living on the Ryukyu Islands, and others try to trace them to what is now called Fukien Province in mainland China. HLA testing has demonstrated that some aborigines are related to the Polynesian peoples in New Zealand; but it is unproved that all are so related. The fact that the various tribes operated independently from each other gives credence to the position that their origins may be of more than one source.

While each group had a unique culture and language, the aborigines were first mistakenly viewed as one nation and called the "Takasago" or High Mountain People" by the Japanese. It was an appropriate name since the central mountain range of Taiwan has 200 peaks over 3,000 meters.

In 1593, the Japanese king, Toyotomi Hideyoshi (豐臣秀吉) dispatched Harada Magoshitiro (原田孫七郎) as an ambassador to this "High Mountain Nation." Hideyoshi sought to invade China and had two routes available; one through Korea and the other through Formosa. Finding that no one tribe in Formosa could representatively speak for all, he chose the route of Korea. It was a bad choice and got Japan involved in an eventual quagmire on that peninsula. When he died in 1598, his campaign was abandoned. If he had gone through Formosa, perhaps Hideyoshi would have fared no better. Regardless, this was the first experience where Formosa was viewed or treated as an independent country by an outsider.

The Name Taiwan

The origins of the name of Taiwan are disputed. Some interpret it as a corruption of the name of the locale (Taoyuan) where the earliest settlements were made. Others see it as the aborigines' name for aliens. When Chinese, Japanese or other aliens came to Formosa, the aborigines people would talk of them as "Taian, or Taiyan" both words which meant "aliens." As often happens in the misunderstanding of language, Dutch traders who later heard these words, associated them with the island and gave Formosa the name Taiwan from these utterances. That same name also appears in the Ming Court's agreement to the occupation of Taiwan by the Dutch.

The Spanish Flag

Ferdinand Magellan, a Portuguese explorer in the service of Spain left there in 1519 in a bold and adventurous attempt to sail around the world. He reached and died in the Philippines in 1521; but one of his five ships would complete this unprecedented adventure by 1523. Encouraged by this voyage, the Spanish returned and by 1565 conquered the Philippines. Spanish interest in Formosa soon developed; they saw it as a midway point between their Philippines settlements and Japan. By occupying Taiwan, they could provide security for the Bashi Channel, share or snatch the Formosan trade from the Dutch and more easily dominate trade routes to Japan. In 1626, despite setbacks in Japan, Spanish fleets from Manila landed on the northeastern coast of Formosa and named the place Santiago. They also entered Keelung and established Fort San Salvador. Two years later they occupied Tamsui on the northwestern coast and established Fort Santo Domingo. Spanish influence was limited to the northern portion of the island. But after seventeen years, they withdrew. Their reasons were many. In addition to being attacked by the Dutch and by the aborigines, many of their soldiers also died of illness. But their main reason for withdrawal was that the samurai government in Japan continued to refuse the Spanish the right to trade and proselytize. As the

Japanese continued to persecute Christians there was little hope that this position would be reversed. Defending Formosa lost its value and the Spanish returned to the Philippines.

The Dutch Flag

While the Spanish were in the Philippines, the Dutch had come to Indonesia in the early 1600's and founded Batavia (Jakarta) in 1619. The Vereenigde Oost-Indische Compagnie (VOC) or United Dutch East India Company, formed in 1602, managed their colonial businesses and trade. In search of a mid-station for their Asian trade, the Dutch traders had already been to the Penghu archipelago (Pescadores) located in the Taiwan Strait in 1603. They had also made repeated attempts to dislodge the Portuguese from Macau but were unsuccessful.

When the Dutch decided to settle in Penghu, their actions drew a quick response from the Ming regime in China. The Ming government had maintained its restrictions on travel abroad and saw this as a threat. They attacked the Dutch on Penghu in 1624. After eight months both sides signed a truce agreement. This agreement had three main points. The Dutch would abandon Penghu; the Ming would not oppose the Dutch occupation of Formosa; and trade would be maintained between the Ming and the Dutch. Since the Ming government did not claim sovereignty over Formosa, this was an easy arrangement for them to make. Following the treaty, the Dutch developed settlements at Anping near Tainan in southwest Taiwan. Soon however they were conscious of the Spanish presence on the north of the island. They also experienced Japanese attempts to establish firm trading bases in Formosa. As a result of this, the Dutch replaced the governor in Batavia and reassigned him as governor of Formosa. From there he could consistently look after Dutch trade activities and interests with both China and Japan.

The Dutch quickly established two forts in the Tainan area. One located at Anping was first called Fort Orange and then Zeelandia. The other, located nearby was called Provintia. Both were capable of defense. Zeelandia housed their trading functions while Provintia housed the administrative, sleeping and warehouse functions. From these solid bases, the Dutch gradually expanded their influence on the island.

Both aborigines and Chinese dwelt near the area where the Dutch settled but they offered little or no opposition. However as the Dutch began to confiscate more land and levy taxes, resentment and resistance slowly built up. In the meantime, the Dutch used missionaries to try to convert the aborigines and using Roman characters translated the Bible into their language. For those who refused to become Christians, the Dutch resorted to military force to drive them from the area. The Dutch also levied a 10% customs duty on all trading in Formosa whether import or export. This 10% duty was opposed by Japanese traders who had been used to trading with the Chinese on Formosa. In 1625, a Japanese sea captain named Hamada Yahiyoue (浜田弥兵衛) refused to pay these taxes and declared himself exempt. This declaration would sour the trade between the Dutch commercial firm in Hirato and the Japanese samurai government. In 1627, Japanese traders brought aborigines leaders to be presented to the Japanese Shogun, but hopes of an alliance were unsuccessful. Finally, trade would temporarily break off when in 1628, Hamada led some aborigines in a failed attempt to assassinate the Dutch governor. An international conflict loomed between the Dutch and Japanese but it dissipated when in 1635 the Tokugawa shogun began a policy of isolationism (sakoku). They forbade trade and then outlawed shipbuilding of ocean going vessels and other ships from 1633—1636. In 1639 they formally entered into a self-imposed isolation policy that would last until 1853 when the "black ships" of Admiral Perry would force their way into Tokyo Bay. With trade down to a trickle and with ship-building hampered, even the Japanese pirate groups lost their influence in the Taiwan Strait.

Dutch Colonial Profit

Using the labor of the aborigines and the Chinese immigrants, the Dutch were quick to gain profit from Formosa. Trade increased. The Dutch could get spices, amber, kapok and opium from Southeast Asia through Batavia. They also got silver from Japan and silk, pottery, Chinese medicine and gold from China. All this was exchanged for sugar, venison and deer hides from Formosa. Formosa was proving valuable to them.

The pirates who surrounded Formosa still existed but the Dutch made a treaty with Cheng Chih-lung (鄭芝龍), a pirate leader, to guarantee the safety of their vessels at sea. The Dutch could now spend time developing agriculture in Formosa. Farmland belonging to the Dutch East India Company was established and immigration encouraged. Immigrants had to pay 5—10% of the profit they made in renting land from the company. The Dutch successfully improved the spice crop and introduced several new crops to the island such as cabbages, garden peas, tomatoes, mangos, capsicum, rice and especially sugarcane. They also brought in the Indian buffalo.

Revolts

During the Dutch rule of the island, there were revolts from the aborigines and Chinese, but the Dutch were able to employ a policy of divide and conquer. The aborigines rose up in the Mattau incident (麻豆事件) in 1635 and the Xiaolung incident (蕭壟事件) in 1636. As these revolts were crushed, the Dutch increased their hold on the island.

The Chinese whose immigration had been openly encouraged also became dissatisfied. In 1652, Guo Huai-i (郭懷一) a subordinate of the pirate Cheng Chih-lung gathered the people together to resist the Dutch. Unfortunately Guo's brother leaked information of the planned revolt to the Dutch and the Dutch with 2000 Christian aborigines met and defeated them.

Lacking appropriate weapons, Guo and 4,000 of his men were routed and hunted down. But this and the other revolts indicated a growing tendency of the various groups on the island to seek their own freedom. They did not look to be united with either China or Japan but simply to be left alone to make a living. In the meantime, the practice of the Dutch to play one side against the other to maintain power, would become a practice among each incoming regime.

Cheng Ch'eng-kung and the Ming Flight

In 1628, the Ming Dynasty found itself with far greater matters of concern than what was happening on Formosa, which had been left to the Dutch. The Manchus in the northeast were expanding their influence and threatening the very existence of the Ming. Seeking both military and capital support, the Ming regime called upon the pirate leader Cheng Chih-lung for help. Chih-lung had been based in Hirato, Japan and had taken a Japanese wife, Tagawa. Chih-lung, who operated both as an opportunistic trader and pirate, was also a mercenary leader with a strong army of followers. The Manchus began their conquest of China in earnest in 1646. They sought to conquer both by using force and enticement. The high officials of the Ming court who had fled south were offered similar positions in the Ch'ing court if they ceased resistance. Chih-lung who posed a military threat was also offered the opportunity to switch sides for a court appointment. Chih-lung's family suspiciously opposed this exchange, but Chih-lung decided to go for the bait and received a comfortable place in Beijing. When Chih-lung later failed to bring his forces along with him, the Manchus placed him under house arrest. Chih-lung's wife Tagawa then committed suicide.

Ch'eng-kung (成功), Chih-lung's son (b. 1624) by Tagawa was away pursuing studies when news of this reached him. He abandoned his studies and having inherited the pirate enterprise from his father he became a scourge to the coastal cities on the east. Ch'eng-kung pledged himself to try to re-establish the Ming rule in China, despite the fact that by not joining his father Chih-lung, he would hasten Chih-lung's execution in 1661.

In 1660, the Manchus ordered all inhabitants of China's east coastal region to move inland 1.728 kilometers, in effect eliminating ports of refuge and supplies for pirates or Ming loyalists. Soon, there were few places on the mainland coast where Ch'eng-kung and his pirates could take refuge except for Kinmen (Quemoy) and the Amoy Islands. It was there that Ch'eng-kung met Ho-Bin (何斌) a translator who had been working for the Dutch East India Company. Ho-Bin told him of the advantages of the island of Formosa.

Formosa, the Ming Invasion

Armed with maps of Formosa supplied by Ho-Bin, Ch'eng-kung set out with a fleet of 400 ships and 25,000 men to take the island. Penghu (the Pescadores) was their first stop. They quickly occupied Penghu and made plans to invade Formosa where the Chinese immigrants who had just suffered defeat in the rebellion of Guo Huai-i were sympathetic to a savior.

Upon landing Ch'eng-kung first seized food supplies for his troops. Then he attacked Fort Provintia because it had fewer defenses. Finally he laid siege to Fort Zeelandia. The Dutch were put in a predicament. They were outnumbered and supplies began to run low. They cried to the governor in Batavia for assistance and to the aborigines, but the distances were too great for sufficient help from Batavia and the aborigines could not muster a strong enough force to break the siege. Eventually after a siege of nine months, they surrendered in 1662. The Dutch had ruled Formosa for 38 years.

After driving out the Dutch, Cheng Ch'eng-kung or Koxinga (Koxinya) as he is called in the West began to plan administrative districts. Though the Dutch had made some divisions of territory, this is the first time that a Chinese system of administration was applied to the island. Ch'eng-kung deliberately chose names to reflect his relationship to the Ming regime.

Formosa was called Dueng-Du (東都), that is the eastern capital of the Ming Regime. Zeelandia was destroyed and the area re-named Anping. The surrounding region (now Tainan) was called Cheng-tien Fu (承天府), which means a government connecting God to his people. To the north, the land was called Tien-sieng (天興縣, flourishing) County, and to the south, Uan-nian (萬年縣, long life) County. A defense bureau named "An-fu" (安撫司, placating) was established in the Pescadore Islands. Ch'eng-kung had used names that reflected the Ming regime's extension.

An immediate problem that Cheng had faced was insufficient food. The population of Formosa during the Dutch rule was one hundred thousand people; Cheng had brought an additional thirty thousand including the soldiers and their families. This rapid increase of population strained the food supply. To resolve this, Cheng confiscated all of the land previously possessed by the Dutch East India Company and transferred it to his regime. These lands were divided among his trusted staff and relatives; and in addition the development of farmland in southern Formosa was aggressively pursued. Cheng unwisely invaded the land that belonged to the aborigines and destroyed any opportunities of peaceful co-existence with them. With the development of the land divided among his staff and relatives, the private land system that has existed into the present was introduced and Cheng's influence expanded from the sea to the land.

Cheng's Death

Less than a year after the taking of Formosa, Cheng died in 1662. He had not realized his goals but a shrine was erected to him by the Chinese immigrants; he was deified and many myths about his life soon developed and spread throughout East Asia. In 1664, feeling pressure from the Manchu people and the Dutch who still traded with China, Cheng Ching (鄭經), the eldest son of Ch'eng-kung who had been left in charge of Amoy, led seven thousand soldiers and their families to Formosa. This marked the Cheng forces complete abandonment of the mainland.

Cheng Ching then proceeded to change and improve the administrative districts set up by his father. He changed

"Dueng-du" to "Dueng-nieng" (東寧, peaceful east); and the two counties became "Tien-sieng Prefecture" and "Uan-nian Prefecture." He further established two more "An-fu" groups on Formosa. "Cheng-tien Fu" was divided into four streets and twenty-four units that were called the "Street Unit System." (坊里制) With this street unit system, Cheng Ching established a census register, which would become the basis of the "Bao-jia System," (保甲制度) a system used for keeping local security. This system is still in use today.

Government affairs were given to Chen Yong-hua (陳永華), the father in law of Cheng Ching's elder son. Yong-hua established many policies for farmland development, education and finance, but he also developed a severe tax system that would make the people feel they were no better off than under the Dutch.

Summary Thought

By 1662, the greater part of Taiwan was still in the hands of the aborigines. Ming loyalists had driven out the Dutch and occupied the south. These loyalists who had chosen Taiwan hoped to use Taiwan as a base to retake the mainland. The Dutch still traded in the area and considered the possibility of retaking the island. The Japanese had become isolationist and retreated to their country. The Spanish had decided to operate from the Philippines. Pirate groups still existed and their chameleon like ability to shift back and forth between pirates and traders made them tolerated. The aborigines begrudgingly shared the island with all as long as the aliens did not encroach too much more on their territory. No one had complete sovereignty over the island.

Questions

There are many methods of determining sovereignty, de facto possession, de jure agreements, historic tradition, a shared mythic destiny, common ethnicity, self-determination etc. In the 20th and 21st centuries which determinations are the most reliable?

Did the Japanese ruler, Toyotomi Hideyoshi view Formosa as a separate kingdom in his invasion of China in 1593 or was he simply seeking to cover his flanks from attack by a third party?

Pirate groups have little or loose national loyalty. Did the pirates of the 16th and 17th centuries consider Formosa their territory or open to those who claimed it?

When the Ming government made its treaty with the Dutch in 1624, was it stating the Pescadores are a part of China, but Taiwan is not? Therefore the Dutch can have it?

How did the Taiwanese aborigines view the Dutch and subsequent presence of other peoples on Taiwan? Did they see each as a tribe occupying the land it could control?

When the Japanese contested the Dutch rights to levy taxes on Taiwan trade, did they consider Taiwan as open territory and not subject to Dutch rule or taxes?

The Spanish, Dutch and other Europeans often claimed lands

in the name of their king or queen. Did they feel that sovereignty was simply a matter of force?

When the pirate Koxinga (Koxinya) took Taiwan from the Dutch did he feel he was breaking the previous Ming treaty? Was he simply seeking a port in a storm and a base for regaining the mainland from the Manchus?

Additional Readings

Anderson, Malcom. *Frontiers*, Polity Press, 1996, Cambridge. How states are formed and the development of the concepts of boundaries and sovereignty.

Campbell, Rev. William. *Formosa under the Dutch,* SMC Publishing Inc., 1992, Tapiei. Written in 1903 it compiles many Dutch diaries and accounts of their rule.

Clough, Ralph N. *Island China*, Harvard University Press,1978, Harvard.

劉其偉, 《台灣原住民文化藝術》, 台北, 雄獅美術, 1997。

潘英, 《台灣平埔族史》, 台北, 南天書局, 1996。

曹永和, 《台灣早期歷史研究》, 台北, 聯經出版社, 1979。

戴天昭, 《台灣國際政治史》, 台北, 前衛出版社, 1996。

彭明敏、黃昭堂合著, 蔡秋雄譯, 《台灣在國際法上的地位》, 台北, 玉山社, 1995。

中村孝志著, 吳密察、翁佳音合編, 《荷蘭時代台灣史研究》, 台北, 稻鄉出版社, 1997。

村上直次郎, 《新港文書 Sinkan Manuscriots》, 台北, 台北帝國大學理農學部, 1933; 台北, 捷幼出版社復刻, 1995。

達帕爾著，施博爾、黃典權譯，〈郭懷一事件〉（收錄於《台灣風物》26卷3期，台北）。

盧千惠，〈郭懷一月夜起義〉（收錄於《新觀念》1998年7月號，台北）。

永積洋子，〈從荷蘭史料來看17世紀的台灣貿易〉（收錄於中央研究院中山人文社科所主辦「第七屆中國海洋發展史國際研討會」論文集，1997，台北）。

《巴達維亞城日記》，台北，台灣省文獻委員會，1970。

《熱蘭遮城日誌》第1冊，台南，台南市政府，2000。

II

The Ch'ing Era

Trouble Within

The Manchus established the Ch'ing Dynasty (1644—1911) and sought ways to eliminate the influence of Cheng Ching and any remnants of the Ming regime. As was mentioned, all people living in the coastal area including Kwangtung, Fukien, Chekiang, Kiangsu and Shantung had to move inland 1.728 km or more. Fishing and trading were forbidden. Naturally as these prohibitions became more severe, smuggling flourished to fill the void.

Formosa became a smugglers' paradise as well as a place of refuge for anyone wanting to flee the Ch'ing regime. The population increased to one hundred and fifty thousand; but so did the development of farmland, so food was not a problem.

While food was not an issue for the people, taxes were. In order to keep their finances high, the Cheng regime on Formosa taxed numerous items, and the suffering of the people which was difficult under the Dutch, became worse. Complaints increased.

In addition to the problem of taxes, another problem developed for the Cheng regime. Cheng Ching, who had taken over from his father, soon got into disputes with his uncle, the younger brother of Ch'eng-kung, over the campaign leadership. In the resulting civil war, Cheng Ching gained victory but in 1681 when he died, another dispute over succession arose between Chen Yong-hua who wanted to focus on managing Formosa and Feng Xi-fan (馮 錫範) and Liou Guo-xvan (劉國軒) who wished to continue the struggle with the Ch'ing regime. Chen Yong-hua supported his son-in-law Ke-chang (克臧), the elder son of Cheng Ching, while Feng and Liou supported Ke-Shuang (克塽), the younger son. After a series of battles, those supporting Ke-Shuang and continuing the war with the Ch'ing won out.

The Ch'ing regime took advantage of these disputes to sow seeds of discontent and distrust among those on Formosa. By 1679, they had set up a building called "Xiou-lai" (修來館, cordial relations) to welcome back anyone belonging to the Cheng camp. Those deserting could receive rewards with the same position and pay that they had had previously. This slowly eroded the strength of the Ming loyalists.

The Empire Strikes

After 1681, the Ch'ing began direct attacks on the Cheng forces. Shi Lang (施琅) was made Naval Superintendent and the chief general in the Formosan Campaign. Shi Lang had been in the Cheng camp and had gone over to the other side after a violent falling out with Ch'eng-kung. The Manchus were primarily mounted land fighters and not familiar with naval fighting. Shi Lang proved to be a valuable asset.

On July 8th 1683, Shi Lang led a fleet of three hundred ships and twenty thousand soldiers to invade the Pescadores. Within one week, he occupied the islands causing panic on Formosa. At Feng Xi-fan's suggestion, Ke-Shuang caved in to the Ch'ing Regime and the Cheng powers sent an envoy to the Pescadores to ask for terms of surrender.

In September, a representative of Shi Lang came to Formosa to accept the seal of the regime and the property lists and to ask the Formosans to adopt the pigtail hairstyle. Shi Lang followed with a large contingent from the Pescadores shortly afterwards and occupied the island without bloodshed. The Cheng Regime, which had ruled since 1662, had come to an end.

Ch'ing Debate

After the Ch'ing regime claimed victory over the Cheng forces, they debated on what to do with Formosa. Two different proposals were put to the imperial court. The majority of advisors suggested that they abandon the troublesome island; but Shi Lang advocated occupying Formosa.

The reasons for abandoning Formosa were simple. It was a small island isolated from China and continued to be a den of pirates, deserters, rebels and criminals fleeing justice. There was no plus side to occupying it. Shi Lang took an opposing view. Formosa had abundant resources that could be utilized; and it could provide a buffer zone or shield to southeast China. Besides, if Formosa was left unattended, the pirates, the Dutch or others could easily return without China being aware of it until it was too late. For these reasons in 1684, the Ch'ing emperor accepted Shi Lang's suggestions to occupy Formosa. So, once again Formosa became involved in the affairs of the mainland.

The Ch'ing's Passive Formosan Policy

At first, the Ch'ing regime took a passive approach to managing Formosa. The primary aim of the government was to occupy it and prevent it from becoming a haven for pirates or anti-government forces. Formosa was put under management of the Fukien Province and divided into three administrative districts, Taiwan Prefecture (台灣縣), the Fengshan Prefecture (鳳山縣) and the Zhuluo Prefecture (諸羅縣) under management of Taiwan Fu (台灣府). Beijing was further concerned lest any kind of local militia would be organized. To control their loyalty, officials and military personnel that were assigned from the mainland to each of these districts were not allowed to bring their families with them to the island. Their average term of duty was to be three years; and they were not allowed to raise troops or provide arms to any of the local people.

At the same time, the Beijing government compelled one hundred thousand Chinese to return to the mainland and passed restrictions on travel to Formosa. Anyone who wished to travel to or visit Formosa needed a special permit from the government and could not bring any family. In this way, the Ch'ing regime sought to control the population of the island, but the stricter their regulations were, the more illegal immigration increased. This happened despite the turbulent seas in the Taiwan Strait, for Formosa provided a place with land and opportunity. Even today boat people, stowaways and smuggled immigrants are a fact of life as people seek better opportunity.

Additional Prohibitions

In order to guard against any future revolutions, the Ch'ing government passed other prohibitions regarding Formosa. The "closed hillsides command" forbade immigrants from entering the regions belonging to the aborigines. Externally, this was to prevent conflicts between the aborigines and immigrants but it also prevented the immigrants from forming any alliance with the aborigines against the government. Boundary lines were established to prevent intermarriage and communications between both groups.

Iron was not allowed to be cast on the island except for the twenty-seven government approved iron casting shops that were designated for making farm tools. Both the making and storage of any weapons were forbidden. Even bamboo, which the immigrants cultivated along their villages for defense, was not allowed to be cut, lest it be used for weapons. But despite these prohibitions, the population increased, agriculture developed and the administrative regions gradually expanded.

Cyclical Revolts Every Three to Five Years

During the next 212 years, over 100 uprisings and revolts are recorded. The people's dissatisfaction with the corrupt officials was the main cause. The military also suffered problems in morale. Military salaries were low and their duties of service were limited to three years so that all looked on their work with a careless attitude. This gave rise to the phrase, "an attempted uprising every three years and a revolt every five years."

Among the more famous revolts in the Ch'ing Regime were the revolt of Chu I-kuei (朱一貴) in 1721, the revolt of Lin Shuang-wen (林爽文) of the Heaven and Earth Society in 1786 and the revolt of Dai Chao-chun (戴潮春) in 1862. In general most of these revolts stemmed from political and economic reasons. Those up to 1786 were usually more political and involved the whole island while those after that year were motivated more by economics and restricted to sections of the island. The weak Formosan garrisons had difficulty with these revolts and often relied on seasoned troops from the mainland to suppress them.

In-fighting between Classes and Groups of People

The Chinese living on Formosa did not feel any strong loyalty to the Ch'ing government or to Formosa, but as immigrants to this land they needed the support and loyalty of others. Their most basic loyalties were to their "brothers" who had come with them from the same prefecture on the mainland or to the sworn brotherhood of a secret society.

One of the greatest of these sworn brotherhoods was that of the "Heaven and Earth Society." This society had two aims. In politics, its purpose was to tear down the Ch'ing regime and restore the Ming; in economy, it formed a popular, mutual self-help organization.

Because of this shared resentment against the Ch'ing as well as sworn brotherhood, whenever any branch of the "Heaven and Earth Society" began a revolt, their action quickly mobilized brothers across the island. Although their organization and mobilization was strong, this group never succeeded in any of its uprisings. A main reason for this failure was the jealous infighting with other groups on the island.

Besides sworn brotherhoods, another competing loyalty among the immigrants was to their place of origin on the mainland. Those from Fukien came from two prefectures, the Chang-chou Prefecture (漳州) and the Ch'uan-chou Prefecture (泉州). Another major group was the Hakka from Kuangtung. These groups had struggled with each other for land and for irrigation water on the mainland and those struggles continued when they came to Formosa. Also competing in this milieu were the aborigines who had their own attachment to the land.

Cooperation among all groups was not easy, and revolts or anti-government actions were weakened by this lack of cooperation. The Ch'ing regime took advantage of these conflicts and could often employ one group against the other. In this way, the Ch'ing kept all groups at bay.

American and European Interest

The 19th Century brought increased interest from foreign imperialists. In 1841 in the midst of the Opium War, English fleets appeared in the vicinity of the island and tried to occupy Keelung Harbor and U-Qi Harbor (梧棲, now called Taichung Harbor) but failed. In 1854, the American fleet, led by Admiral Matthew Calbraith Perry anchored off of Keelung for ten days. Using the excuse of searching for a missing sailor, they landed on Formosa and investigated the potential of mining the coal deposits in that area. Perry, who had opened up Japan to the West, emphasized in reports that Formosa provided a convenient, mid-way trade location and was very defensible. It could serve as a base for exploration in a similar way as Cuba had done for the Spanish in the Americas, and could help counter European monopolization of the trade routes.

The United States government ignored Perry's suggestions to claim sovereignty over the island but his reports attracted European powers. In the Tientsin Treaty (天津條約) of 1858 the Ch'ing government agreed to open up four harbors on Formosa to America, England, France and Russia. The two main harbors were Anping and Tamsui; two lesser harbors were Keelung and Takao (Kaohsiung). The ports of Taiwan became active with trading ships.

In addition the Ch'ing formally allowed westerners to preach Christianity on Formosa. The Spanish and Dutch had brought the

Christian faith to the island; but each country preferred its own missionaries who might also look after its interests. Among the new church groups was the English Presbyterian Church in 1865 and seven years later the Canadian Presbyterian Church.

The Tientsin Treaty soon brought additional foreign merchants to the island and created conflicts between the foreigners and the local residents. Pressured by complaints, a new agreement was signed in 1868 between the Ch'ing government and the western powers. This agreement gave further concessions to the foreigners including the following:

1) The local monopoly on camphor was abolished and the market opened to foreigners.
2) The government would forbid slanderous talk against Christianity.
3) Foreign merchants would be allowed to travel freely on Formosa.

From this time on, the economy of Formosa became more and more global. Formosan tea and camphor were exported from Tamsui and Keelung and sugar was exported from Anping and Takao. In the meantime both opium and food supplies were imported into Formosa.

Japanese Interest Revives

After the Meiji Restoration in Japan in 1868, Japan came out of isolation. Disputes began between the Japanese and Ch'ing governments over the territorial sovereignty of the Ryukyus, an island kingdom in the East China Sea. This kingdom included present-day Okinawa, Amami and Sakishima.

In 1871, the Miyako, a ship from the Ryukyu kingdom, foundered off the southeast coast of Formosa and sixty-six people came ashore. Upon their landing on the island, aborigines of the Peony Tribe and other tribes killed fifty-four of the people. The remaining twelve escaped and eventually got safe passage back to the Ryukyus.

The next year, the Meiji government of Japan assigned Kabayama Sukenori (樺山資紀) and Mizuno-Jyun (水野遵) to come to Formosa and begin an investigation. Charles W. LeGendre a retired American Consul from Amoy, China was also in this party. LeGendre had been hired as an advisor by the Meiji government because of his international experience in dealing with foreign shipping accidents. He had also successfully negotiated a settlement of a similar incident between aborigines and American sailors.

The Ch'ing government sought to escape international responsibility by maintaining that their sovereign rights did not extend to the aboriginal areas. As a result, LeGendre used this claim to directly negotiate a shipping succor treaty with the chief of the aborigines. In this way he established that there were two authorities coexisting on Formosa; the West Side controlled by the Ch'ing and the East Side by the aborigines.

In March of 1873, Soejima Taneomi (副島種臣) arrived in Beijing to negotiate with the Ch'ing government for reparations. LeGendre anticipated that the Ch'ing government would continue to try to escape international responsibility and encouraged the Japanese to attack the location of the Peony tribe. So in April 1874, the Meiji government dispatched Saigo Tsugumichi (西鄉 從道) and Okuma Shigenobu (大隈重信) to lead troops against Formosa. They left Nagasaki on May 17th and landed successfully near Hengchun (恆春) on May 22nd. The Japanese set up camps and sought reparation from the aborigines. The Ch'ing government responded to what could be seen as an invasion. However, by sending Shen Bao-zhen (沈葆楨) with an army to confront the Japanese on Formosa it was accepting some responsibility. Tensions grew.

In the meantime, the Americans and English, fearful that a conflict between the Ch'ing and the Japanese would harm their trade profits, pressed for a peaceful solution. With their mediation, peace was forthcoming but the Japanese would obtain many concessions.

In a special treaty made in 1874 in Beijing, the Ch'ing government agreed to pay both compensation to the families of the victims and construction expenses to the Japanese for their contribution to Formosa (the dwellings and roads built in their six months on the island). The Chinese also admitted that the Japanese were justified in dispatching their troops to protect their citizens, thus recognizing the people from the Ryukyu Islands as Japanese citizens. This in turn resolved the territorial disputes over those islands and the Ryukyu Islands were officially recognized as belonging to Japan. The Chinese termed this "the Peony Tribe Affair;" it proved to be a costly affair for the Ch'ing.

Changes in the Ch'ing Formosan Policy

After the Peony Tribe Affair, the Ch'ing government began to reconsider its Formosan policy. It assigned Shen Bao-chen to come to Formosa and strengthen its defenses. In beginning some reforms, Shen became more aggressive in management of the island and made the following changes.

1) The prohibition forbidding contact between immigrants and aborigines was canceled.
2) Restrictions on immigration were lifted and it was openly encouraged.
3) Administrative districts were reorganized and increased.
4) Fukien Province's senior officer must spend six months of each year living in Formosa.
5) Military affairs were reorganized.
6) Foreign engineers were hired to open the coalmines.
7) A road connecting east and west was built across the central mountain range.
8) A postal service was developed to accelerate transference of official documents.

Shen set great ideals of reform but because he remained in Formosa for less than a year, these were not fully put into practice.

Another reformer Ding Ri-chang (丁日昌) replaced him and attempted to set up electric cable communications between Formosa and the mainland and to construct a railroad between Keelung and Hengchun. But Ding's stay was also too short to complete his plans and as a result all changes were partially carried out.

The French Flag, a Brief Moment

After the Tientsin Treaty of 1858, the French also developed an interest in Formosa. In April 1884, the French and the Ch'ing regime entered war over the sovereignty of Vietnam and this spilled over into Formosa. French fleets anchored off of Keelung attacked both Keelung and then Tamsui. French troops landed. In the following year, France concluded an armistice with the Ch'ing government and received concessions in Vietnam. Graves of the French military who died in this war can still be found in Keelung and Penghu as a memory of this time.

The brief invasion by French troops, however, made the Ch'ing government more acutely aware of the importance they needed to pay to Formosa. Liu Ming-chuan (劉銘傳) was assigned to Formosa to accelerate the previously abandoned policies.

Provincial Status

One of the important achievements of Liu Ming-chuan was to request the Ch'ing court to allow Formosa to become independent of Fukien; and in October 1885 Formosa was officially granted provincial status. It was called Taiwan Province and Liu became the first governor of the province. With this provincial status, Taiwan began to have a growing sense that though it contained separate societies, groups and peoples, it was one.

Liu's first task was to reorganize the administrative districts, which he did with such foresight that they would be the basis for the succeeding periods both under the Japanese, and the KMT. Over thirty new institutions were developed to handle governmental affairs such as the tax bureau, the agrarian investigation bureau, the railroad bureau, the tea, salt, coal and many other bureaus.

The Return of a Passive Policy

Despite the foreign interest in Formosa and its growing importance, it continued to be a backwater assignment to court officials in Beijing. No official appointed to Formosa sought to remain there. In June of 1891, Liu would use ill health as an excuse for leaving Formosa and Shao Iou-lian (邵友濂) would be appointed to replace him as provincial governor. Shao's style of government was much more passive and the reformation policies soon lapsed back into a stage of neglect.

Shao's main contribution would be to move the capital from Tainan to Taipei where it has remained, thus beginning the dominance of the north as the political center. Shao would in turn leave in December 1894 and Tang Zieng-sung (唐景崧) would replace him. But before Tang had any chance to be effective, trouble was brewing in Korea.

A Brief Flirtation with Democracy

Japan and China had both been seeking to dominate Korean politics. In 1894—95, this dispute would finally erupt in a war that Japan would quickly win. In the following Treaty of Shimonoseki, Japan would receive Taiwan, Penghu and the Liaotung peninsula as concessions. Though western powers would pressure Japan to surrender the Liaotung peninsula and Russia would gain influence there, Taiwan and Penghu had now become a part of Japan. The articles of the treaty agreement between the Ch'ing government and Japan shocked the people of Formosa. Particularly poignant was the fact that the people learned the news not from the Ch'ing government but from foreign traders coming to the island. The people wondered how a battle that took place in the northern corners of China was their affair. They asked how a defeat in the north could mean giving away territory in the south. Traditionally the Chinese have considered any foreign countries including Japan as barbarian. For the educated Formosans, that the Japanese would have sovereignty over the island seemed unthinkable. Some of the gentry sought then to make Formosa independent from the Ch'ing government and its decisions. They decided to establish a new country called the Taiwan Republic. With little background on the concept of democracy, the people still desired to establish a democratic state based on self-determination. Their closest model was the country of Alsace-Lorraine located between France and Germany and a part of German territory after the Franco-Prussian War of 1870—1871.

The Formosan gentry forced the Provincial Governor Tang to accept their plan and made him president of the new country, the Taiwan Republic. In May 1895, this new country was declared and all foreign consulates in Taiwan were notified. Also called the Formosan Republic it established a national flag, stamps, a great seal and an official reigning title of Yueng-Ch'ing (永清). In case the Ch'ing government returned this title meant that the people were still loyal to the Ch'ing. While the gentry covered their bases with this, the common people were prepared to go their own way.

The new democracy appointed its officers. Tang Ching-sung would be President; Qiou Feng-jia (邱逢甲) would be Vice President and Militia Commander; Yu Mieng-zhen (俞明震) would be Minister of Domestic Affairs; Cheng Ji-tueng (陳季同) would be Minister of Diplomatic Affairs; Lin Uei-yvan (林維源) would be Head of Parliament, and so forth. A full cabinet was established. Nevertheless when the Japanese came, none of the members had the fortitude to live and die for Taiwan.

Most of them like Tang had been forced to remain on Taiwan by the gentry. As Japanese occupation loomed, Lin Uei-yvan offered to buy his way out of this local office with a substantial amount of money and many of the others sought to leave. All soon disappeared to Amoy after fighting broke out. The Taiwan Republic's government quickly vanished after only three months of existence. But while the government's life was short, the concept of "all of us here are Taiwanese" was born and began to develop among the common residents of Taiwan.

Taiwan's Value for Japan

At the time of the Peony Tribe affair, the American Charles W. LeGendre had encouraged the Japanese government to possess Formosa to secure Japan's imperial state. Japanese intellectuals like Hukuzawa Yukiti also emphasized the importance of possessing Formosa from the standpoint of national defense. Such theories saw Formosa as an important buffer for Japan's southern coast. How or whether these recommendations directly influenced Japan's East Asian policy is difficult to confirm, but knowingly or unknowingly, Formosa became a part of Japan.

At the end of 1894, Inoue Kowashi, who had served as education minister in 1893, also submitted opinions to Prime Minister Ido Hirobumi on the importance of Formosa as part of Japanese defense. Further, in 1895, Nakamura Zyunkuro, a naval professor, sought to persuade the naval commander Kabayama Sukenori that the government should make Formosa part of Japan because of its geographical position at the entrance of the South China Sea.

In addition to national defense, the Japanese intelligentsia considered their expanding population. Hukuzawa Yukiti (福澤諭吉), Tokutomi Sohou (德富蘇風), Riku Katsunan (陸羯南), Taguti Ukiti (田口卯吉) and others publicly proclaimed that Japan after defeating the Ch'ing in 1895 should use Formosa to resolve their agricultural and peasant problems. The island could produce both an abundance of crops and be a place for expansion.

Thus, in March 1895, Japan assigned troops to both occupy

Penghu and blockade Taiwan. Then in May of the same year, Japan formally took over the sovereignty of the island from the Ch'ing government. The era of Japanese rule was about to begin.

Summary Thought

By 1895 Taiwan had attracted the notice of several countries, and the Ch'ing which had at first neglected Taiwan changed its position. Some improvements were begun but they were not far-reaching since appointed government officials always sought to leave as soon as they could arrange it. The common people felt more loyalty to their brotherhoods or place of origin than to the Ch'ing government, but this was the case even on the mainland.

Foreign powers once again cast covetous eyes on Taiwan as a base of operations for trade. The Japanese broke their isolationism and also saw the value of Taiwan to their country. With all this growing interest, the Ch'ing government which at first only claimed sovereignty over the western side of the island, saw it was in their best interest to claim the whole island. Taiwan received provincial status. Ten years after this provincial status, China would give Taiwan to the Japanese "in perpetuity."

Questions

Can the frequent revolts on Taiwan be viewed as people protesting hard times and simply seeking to be left alone? Or were the people seeking true self-determination?

Were the European powers' ambitions toward Taiwan territorial and therefore sovereign? Or did these powers just seek a guaranteed location for trading with China?

Why did western countries always bring missionaries to any place they colonized? Did this have anything to do with aims at sovereignty?

What was the value of Taiwan getting provincial status?

While Ch'ing attitudes toward the value and status of Taiwan changed, why was being assigned there still more of an exile than an appointment?

The Ch'ing government admitted that it did not control the territory occupied by the aborigines. Had any government up to that time ever completely controlled Taiwan?

What were the ramifications of the Taiwan Republic declaring itself an independent republic?

Was the Japanese purpose in acquiring Taiwan expansionist or protectionist?

Additional Readings

Davidson, James W. *The Island of Formosa, Past and Present*, 1972, Taipei. This work, originally written in 1903, has extensive quotes of correspondence and foreign transactions concerning Taiwan during the Ch'ing period.

Struve, Lynn A. *The Southern Ming, 1644–1662*, Yale Univ. Press,

1984, New Haven. Intrigue and changing loyalties during the Ch'ing takeover.

郁永河，《裨海紀遊》，台北，眾文圖書公司。

陳純瑩，《明鄭對台灣的經營》，台北，台灣師範大學歷史研究所碩士論文，1986。

王詩琅，《清廷台灣棄留之議》，高雄，德馨室出版社，1979。

林榮梓，《台灣歷史啓示錄》，台北，觀音山出版社，1996。

尹章義，《台灣開發史研究》，台北，聯經出版公司，1989。

張勝彥，〈清代台灣漢人土地所有型態之研究〉（收錄於氏著《台灣史研究》），台北，華世出版社，1981。

謝國興，《官逼民反～清代台灣三大民變》，自立報系出版部，1993。

林偉盛，〈清代台灣分類械鬥發生的原因〉（收錄於張炎憲等編《台灣史論文精選》），台北，玉山社，1996。

戴寶春，《清季淡水開港之研究》，台北，台灣師範大學歷史研究所專刊，1984。

陳志奇，《中國近代外交史》，台北，南天書局，1993。

鄭連明編，《台灣基督長老教會百年史》台北，台灣基督長老教會印行，1965。

藤井志津枝，《近代中日關係史源起1871～74年台灣事件》，台北，金禾出版社，1992。

毛利敏彥，《台灣出兵》，東京，中央公論社，1996。

黃昭堂，《台灣民主國の研究》，東京，東京大學出版會，1970。

吳密察，《台灣近代史研究》，台北，稻鄉出版社，1994。

III

The Japanese Era

The Japanese Flag

Taiwan was Japan's first official colony; and with it, Japan entered a new sphere of international politics. It had already begun its industrial revolution, but now it could claim parity with western countries as a colonial power. The Japanese were eager that all would go well. Kabayama Sukenori was appointed Governor of Taiwan and Mizuno Zyun as Minister of Civil Administration. Both left for Taiwan on May 24th 1895, and arrived on May 29th, the same day that Japanese troops landed on the island. The ceremony for reception of the government however was held on board a ship on June 2nd because of threats of disruptions from the Taiwanese and potential intervention by foreign authorities.

These fears may have been exaggerated. The newly formed army of the Taiwan Republic, numbering fifty to a hundred thousand, would provide some initial resistance in the north but they were quickly routed. As for the foreign powers, France, though interested, was occupied with Madagascar and could not spare any troops. England had little opportunity or cause. The English already had access to trade in Taiwan so Hong Kong would remain their focus.

The Collapse of Taiwan's Republic

The leaders of Taiwan's Republic movement and its soldiers began to abandon the republic shortly after the fighting began. President Tang fled to the island of Amoy off the coast of Fukien on June 19th and others soon followed. Tang's flight earned him the questionable title of the "Ten Day President" since that was the duration of his stay after the establishment of the Taiwan Republic.

The original provincial appointments of Taiwan's leaders had come from the Beijing government but the treaty nullified those positions. Though the leaders now had new positions leading the Taiwan Republic, supposedly they had no salary with these positions. It would test their personal commitment and leaving was their answer. The new government of the Taiwan Republic collapsed with their departure.

Still, there were others willing to sacrifice for Taiwan. Since the Japanese easily occupied the northern part of the island, the Japanese anticipated that it would not be long before they controlled the whole island. They were mistaken.

Taipei had been easy to capture since the majority of the people viewed it as a place of business and not home. People had little personal commitment to Taipei and in some ways the Japanese were welcomed. The Japanese could keep law and order in the streets and business could continue. But the south was a different story.

The majority of the island's residents including forty-five thousand aborigines and two hundred and fifty five thousand Chinese immigrants lived in central and southern Taiwan. This is where their ancestral homes were; they would do their utmost to prevent Japanese rule there.

Bandits?

Chinese residents were initially told that they would have two years (until May 8, 1897) to consider remaining on the island and becoming Japanese subjects or selling their possessions and moving elsewhere in the world. Less than 1% of the population, around 4,000—6,000 residents, would choose to leave, Taiwan was their home for better or worse.

As a result, resistance continued even though the new government folded. It would take the Japanese five months to suppress the fighting and uprisings, and in the struggles that followed, some fourteen thousand residents would die.

What was surprising in this struggle was that the Chinese and the aborigines fought together. A sense of a "Taiwanese" consciousness was developing among these longtime foes as they tried to stop the Japanese. They were called "bandits," by the Japanese and their most violent resistance came from Yunlin (雲林), Chiayi (嘉義) and the surrounding areas.

In 1898, Godou Shinpei (後藤新平), the fourth civil administrator of Taiwan, decided to use an iron hand to solve the "bandit" problem. He expanded the police force and made full use

of the "Bao-jia System" that had long been in practice during the
Ch'ing regime. The colonial government also created "bandit
laws" resulting in the punishment of 32,000 Formosans under this
category. That was over 10% of the population of the island at the
time.

Laying the Foundations of Japanese Rule

According to the 63rd code of the Japanese Imperial Diet, the
governor general of Taiwan was given the powers of administration, legislation, justice, military and education. Such a wide range
of authority and privileges violated the legislative authority of the
Imperial Diet. Nevertheless, this special arrangement would
continue until 1921 when the colonial government's legislative
authority reverted back to the Imperial government.

There were two schools of thought in the Imperial government
as to how the island should be ruled. One school favored direct
assimilation, and preferred that all the laws and systems of
Imperial Japan should be imposed on the island at once. The other
school favored a gradual assimilation with the tempo being
determined by changing circumstances. These disputes would
continue for some time.

In June of 1898, as Godou served under the fourth general
governor, Kotama Gentarou (兒玉源太郎), he executed a policy
called "biological colonial management." He borrowed the term
from biology, and explained it with the following comparison.
"Just as you don't move the eyes of a flounder to a bream, so you

don't automatically move one country's rules and policies to its colony."

Examining Cultural Practices

In keeping with the policy of "biological colonial management," many kinds of exploratory studies were begun. Before transplanting their culture into Taiwan, the Japanese examined the climate, lifestyles and customs of Taiwan to see how their culture would best be adapted to it.

The Japanese knew that the western world, which had had its own colonial problems, would be watching Taiwan. Nervous and conscious of such attention, the Japanese Diet had even toyed with the idea of selling Taiwan to France but decided it was in their best interests to keep it. They would transplant their culture cautiously.

In 1898, a temporary "Agrarian Investigation Bureau" was set up and the traditional dual owner agrarian system was revoked. The colonial government successfully transferred agrarian ownership from the nominal landowners to the people that actually tilled the soil and worked in the fields. Furthermore, all "open territory" was declared national property. The government then sold this national property to retired Japanese officers and enterprises at a cheaper price to encourage settlement and investment in Taiwan. The Japanese were changing the structures of the economy.

In 1901, the "Ancient Taiwanese Customs Investigation

Bureau" was established. Godou Shinpei served as the first president and invited scholars into the bureau to do research and analysis on Taiwanese traditional customs. The work of this bureau provided valuable insights into and understanding of the traditional Chinese lifestyle and is still referenced today.

A census was carried out in 1905, the first time a census had been held on Taiwan. At that time there were 3,040,000 registered people living on the island, 97.8% of whom were Formosan and 1.89% were Japanese; but the statistics were not completely accurate since it was difficult to register both "bandits" and aborigines.

Infrastructure Development

Under Godou, many programs were instigated; he himself had majored in the medical field and found that little attention had been paid to hygiene and medicine on the island. Thus, one of his first projects was for health and medical treatment. He recommended an English technician, W. K. Burton to come to Taiwan to construct waterworks and a sewer system. Godou also promoted the establishment of medical schools and hospitals throughout the island.

To promote the free flow of trade, finance and the development of industry, the colonial government set out to unify the currency and establish a Taiwan Bank to publish bank notes and government bonds. The Taiwan Bank also established branches at Amoy, Shantou, Guangzou, Shanghai and Hong Kong. This set the foundation for capitalistic development on Taiwan.

Infrastructure development also continued in postal service, telecommunications, shipping, harbors, railways and highways. Programs were begun or accelerated in development. To insure construction funds, the colonial government issued bonds.

One result of the improved travel and communications around the island was a greater shared consciousness among the many regions of Taiwan. The five major rivers of Taiwan that had by nature divided the island into separate sections were bridged, thereby unifying the island in a way not previously done. Trade between regions that had previously gone by way of Amoy could now be direct.

Agriculture became the focal point of industry, especially the growing of rice and sugar cane. Godou invited the agriculturist Isonaga Yoshi (磯永吉) to improve the quality of the rice crops. He also invited Nitobei Inazou to Taiwan to develop technology for refining sugar. By the end of 1900, a new type of refined sugar factory, the Taiwan Refined Sugar Company, was established in Tainan.

Financially, the independence of the colonial government was reached by 1905, and Yanaihara Tadao (矢內原忠雄), an economics professor at Tokyo University was quoted as saying that "Taiwan is Japan's most valuable colony as far as finance and economy is concerned." The life style and economic range of Taiwan gradually expanded and deepened.

Amidst this development, a growing consciousness of being different from the mainland and of being Taiwanese was developing. The people were treated differently from the Japanese, so they could not find identity there. They were also isolated from affairs on the mainland; their identity would be their own.

Changing Forms of Resistance

Initially, resistance to Japan had been armed, and active warfare was conducted in defense of the Taiwan Republic. This had been crushed by November 1895 and direct resistance changed to guerrilla warfare. Guerrilla warfare would be suppressed by 1902 and a lull would ensue. Then in 1905 a third form of protest began that was markedly different from the first two. This stage was characterized by responses to the changing economy. People's previously accepted ways of earning an income were being lost.

Opposition to change and the impact of modern developments can be found in any nation-state; such social opposition can also easily be associated with negative behavior in resisting imperialism. Those who resist modern advances are classified as social malcontents.

When the colonial government promulgated laws and decrees for industrial development, many with vested interests were affected and rose in protest. Their issues became linked with national causes. The unemployed and those who lost the right to use land that had been public vented their frustration by rebellion.

An example of this was the Beipou Affair (北埔事件) in 1907, in which protesters resisted the monopolization of the camphor industry by Japanese enterprises. The Linkipo Affair (林杞埔事件) in 1912 was against the nationalization and sale of timberland. This open property was sold to the Mitsubishi Paper Manufacturing Company at a very low price. The Davani affair (噍吧哖事件) in 1915, viewed as a matter of national identity and religion by some researchers, was simply a case where Taoist protesters sought sanctuary in a temple. Throughout, the people were dissatisfied with the takeover of land or the loss of land that they had previously used under squatter's rights or as open territory.

For example, many people would cut and sell the bamboo from the mountain land that the government sold to Mitsubishi. Mitsubishi subsequently fenced that land off. Even land that had been claimed by certain families was seized if the people did not have resident dwellings, proof of ownership or could not afford to get court records. People who lost their ownership of land or the use of land found it difficult to adapt and make a living in this new modern society. Protest and riots resulted.

Using the System

After 1920, the method of resistance gradually changed due to the education of the people. Several of the younger generation had accepted modern education and had had chances for further studies in Japan. Their studies exposed them to the social movements and civil rights issues prevalent in Japan and the rest of the world. These Taiwanese saw that there could be a way to work within the system for change.

Students who studied in Tokyo and were part of the upper class organized circles like Xingmen Hui (新民會) or the new civilian party, and published a magazine, *Taiwanese Youth,* that promoted the goal of social reformation and the welfare of Taiwan. Their thoughts stressed the ideas of an elite class on the island. As a result of these ideas, new groups and movements linked with national identity began to flourish.

On January 30th 1921, some of the elite expressed the desire to establish Taiwanese participation in the Japanese Imperial Diet. This aspiration gradually took the form of a formal petition to pursue the establishment of a Taiwanese assembly; it would repeatedly be made for fourteen years. In 1923, after the petition was presented for the third time, the colonial government decided to put the clamps on it. The elite were accused of fomenting trouble and violating "the Decrees of Police Security".

The only concrete crime that these people could be accused of was the "establishment of an organization for the Taiwanese assembly." Ninety-nine people were arrested and their homes were searched. Twelve people were sentenced at a second trial even though at the first trial, Judge Holida Masaru (堀田眞猿) had proclaimed the verdict of not guilty. Their term of imprisonment was set at three to four months.

As the common people watched the elite heading to prison, they cheered and gave them moral support. After their release from prison, these members continued to send in their petition for the Taiwanese assembly. Their efforts harmonized with the establishment of the "Taiwan Cultural Association."

Traditional violent resistance had now gradually transformed into modern political social change. Through their own efforts, the people were working hard to enter the Japanese Diet. Because the Japanese government was open to enlightened thought at this time, these practices became the largest in scale and longest exercise of political determination in the Japanese Era.

A Sense of a Taiwanese Culture

There were other social developments such as the "Taiwan Cultural Association" established in October of 1921. Many intellectuals realized that the only way to enlighten the Taiwanese people on how to pursue their own rights was to educate them. As a result, this organization began a series of activities that included: 1) publishing a newsletter, 2) establishing a small library with newspapers for the common people to read, 3) holding lectures, 4) conducting summer school for those who wished to learn more, 5) providing various speeches on culture via a mobile forum around the island, 6) promoting cultural plays on stage and 7) providing cultural films for people around the island. Speeches on all social topics were the most popular, and from 1925–26 over 230,000 attended such presentations.

Other Social Movements

The Taiwan Cultural Association worked more in the countryside and among the people; it became involved in the start of the peasant and labor movements. In the latter part of the 1920's, the far left began to influence and infiltrate such social movement in Taiwan. In June of 1926, the Taiwan Peasant Association was established and became the largest peasant organization on the island. In February and April of 1928, the Taiwan Laborers Association and Taiwan Communist Party were respectively established.

The original members of the Taiwan Cultural Association were of the landowner class, but successive new members came from the working or proletarian classes and gained status in the organization. As a result, in August 1930, elite members such as Lin Xian-tang (林獻堂), Cai Pei-huo (蔡培火), Jiang Wei-shui (蔣渭水) and Yang Zhao-jia (楊肇嘉) decided to leave and found another group called the "Taiwan Local Autonomy Association." This organization sought self-determination on a local level. The Taiwan Cultural Association, which was more and more influenced by left-wing members, opposed the Taiwan Local Autonomy Association and its right-wing thought.

The Taiwan Local Autonomy Association recognized the contributions of the colonial authority and strove for the welfare of the Taiwanese. As a result, from 1931 on, while colonial authority began to clamp down on the left, the Taiwan Local Autonomy

Association was able to continue until 1937 when war broke out between Japan and China.

Taiwan's Communist Party

In the 1920's communism was attracting followers in numerous nations around the world, and Taiwan was no exception. The Taiwanese Communist Party was established in April 1928; people like Xie Xve-hueng (謝雪紅), Lin Mu-shuen (林木順), and Ueng Ze-sheng (翁澤生) had met in secret across the Strait at Shanghai. Initially it was a branch of the Japanese Communist Party and accepted the instructions of the International Communist Party. It had thirteen objectives. It would 1) oppose Japanese imperialism, 2) support Taiwan's independence, 3) establish a Republic of Taiwan, 4) abolish all laws that suppressed the peasantry and labor class, 5) establish a seven hour work day, 6) establish the freedom to strike, assemble, form associations, speak openly and to publish, 7) classify all land as for the poor peasants, 8) abolish feudal authority, 9) develop laws for unemployment insurance, 10) oppose all laws harmful to the proletariat, 11) advocate relations with the Soviet Union, 12) promote a revolution in China and 13) oppose any wars of the new imperialism.

The Taiwanese Communist Party soon split because of different ideologies and strategies. Xie Xve-hueng, a female communist leader, thought that the Party should be involved in the activities of other legal social organizations to cover its illegal status. Ueng Ze-sheng and other young communists opposed this route, but Xie's method predominated, so many of the social movements took on a definite leftist inclination as the communists infiltrated them.

There were three stages to these civil rights and social movements. First in the early 1920's, they were concerned with the issue of national identity; then in the second half of the 1920's they developed proletarian exercises or practices; finally after the 1930's, they went underground as Japanese opposition allowed only those social movements that supported local autonomy.

Outside Taiwan, world events would once again affect the island. In 1937, the incident at the Marco Polo Bridge outside Beijing would escalate into war between Japan and China, and in September the colonial government would stop all social movements.

The Mu-Sha Affair and the Aborigines

Amidst these social developments, the Japanese worked at controlling the whole island, and this included areas that were previously the domain of the aborigines. Naturally this met with resistance.

When the Japanese took over Taiwan, 70 to 80% of the camphor production in the world came from Taiwan. The source of camphor was almost always high in the mountains where the aborigines lived. If the Japanese colonial authority wished to control this resource of camphor, it was imperative that they secure the mountain regions.

To this end, the colonial government developed policies to control the life and actions of the aborigines. Japanese policemen were assigned to live in the mountain regions; they were given power to garrison, administrate and educate. They also had authority to force aborigines to do construction work. The police were encouraged to marry and settle down. Many policemen took advantage of these powers to exploit the labor of the aborigines and intermarry with aboriginal women to their advantage. While the policy had benefits and brought medical and educational functions along with it, more friction and troubles were created between the Japanese and aborigines.

Resistance exploded into violence on October 27th 1930. At the flag-raising ceremony for the Mu-Sha (霧社) elementary school sport meet, the aborigines staged an uprising. They swarmed onto the field and massacred 132 Japanese (and 2 Chinese present), and injured 215 Japanese. The 2 Chinese were killed in error because they were wearing Japanese outfits.

The colonial government responded by assigning an army composed of two thousand seven hundred soldiers, police and Chinese youth to suppress this movement. Six aboriginal communities were involved in the riot and it took fifty days to end the Mu-Sha affair. Over two hundred and seventy six people had died and the aborigines living in the Mu-Sha area had to relocate their villages to another area.

The Mu-Sha affair caused severe shock waves to ripple through the colonial authority, yet the ever-tightening strength of the Japanese forces would eventually bring about calm. The aborigines would continue to use the Japanese language; it even became more popular among them than with the Chinese immigrants. They would also go on to join the Japanese army and fight throughout Southern Asia during World War II. Overall the Japanese methods were successful; but the Mu-Sha affair cast doubts on the government's strategy.

World War II Interrupts All

As was seen earlier, outside events again influenced the island. After Japan took over Manchuko in northeast China, Japan became isolated from the West. In March 1933 it withdrew from the League of Nations. After September 1936, the whole Empire, including Taiwan became involved in wartime preparations. The Japanization and industrialization of Taiwan and its development as a southern base for expansion became the new goals of the colonial government.

The process of Japanization aimed at strengthening national assimilation. The colonial authority prohibited Chinese characters from being printed in the newspapers and promoted the use of the Japanese language. The people were asked to pay their respects to the Japanese shrines. All Taiwan's traditional customs were stopped and the people were encouraged to change their names to Japanese ones.

After 1940, all established social organizations could continue for only two reasons, either to strengthen the wartime system or promote the assimilation of Formosans into becoming real Japanese subjects. Training centers in agriculture, industry, harbor facilities, merchant marine, shipping and oceanography were used to develop the young men to be conscious of Japan's development of Southeast Asia.

In harmony with Japan's national policy, the Taiwan Development Company with thirty-two branches was established in Asia with capital that was one half government and one half local. Most of the company's investment was directed to Taiwan and parts of southern China and Southeast Asia which were occupied by the Japanese army. Areas of investment included the development of uncultivated lands, colonial management, industry, business, mining, transportation, entertainment and securities.

Taiwan was developed as a military base and springboard for southern operations. Industry that would support the military was quickly developed. Modern industries including steel, chemical, fiber, metal and machinery prospered. By March of 1944, the industrial manufacturing output was over seven hundred million-yen, the highest achieved. To keep pace with this industrialization, the infrastructure of the island continued to expand and develop. Agriculture also improved to produce enough food for the battle front.

As the Japanese battle lines extended, more and more troops were needed. From April 1942 until 1944, the colonial authority recruited over six thousand Taiwanese volunteers and assigned them to the front, among them were over one thousand eight hundred aborigines. From this time on, Taiwan was directly involved in the war; it would even have prisoner of war camps for Allied prisoners captured throughout the Pacific Theater.

Taiwanese continued to be drafted into the army. In September of 1944, an additional twenty-two thousand were enlisted by conscription. While this was taking place, the electoral law of the House of Representatives was revised in March of 1945. Taiwan could now assign two Senators and elect five of its own as Members of Parliament in the Japanese Diet. But these civil and political rights that had been adamantly sought came too little, too late, as the war was hastening to its end and Japan would be forced to give up Taiwan.

All in all, some two hundred thousand people, including nurses, technicians, farmers and military personnel, had entered the war effort and thirty thousand had died. When the war ended, other troubles would ensue. The Taiwanese lost their Japanese nationality; they lost representation; and the issue of wartime victim compensation would become a problem for them.

Independence after the War?

When Japan was defeated, most Taiwanese struggled to grasp the defeat's full meaning. The defeat affected them as well as the Japanese. In one sense, it meant that the Taiwanese were liberated from fifty years of colonial rule. In another sense, China, which had been the "enemy state," had suddenly become the "mother country" and those on Taiwan found themselves with mixed and complicated emotions.

Some Japanese military personnel could not face the reality of defeat and attempted to cooperate with those on Taiwan who sought independence. A newly established organization, the Taiwan Social Security Keeping Organization (TSSKO, 台灣治安維持會) asked the colonial governor general Andou Rikiti (安藤利吉) to declare independence. Andou however opposed Taiwan's independence as well as its autonomy and so the plan was halted in its tracks. Nevertheless, any Taiwanese members of the TSSKO immediately became suspect and would be placed in prison by the incoming KMT government for one to two years. Andou would be captured by the Allies and would commit suicide while he was being sent to Shanghai to be tried as a war criminal.

Approximately 480,000 Japanese (military and civilian) personnel were living on Taiwan when the war ended. Some 200,000 of these wished to remain in Taiwan after the war but were refused so by the KMT government. With the exception of 28,000 technical personnel, all Japanese were ordered to leave before April 1946. In leaving, each was allowed to take only one thousand yen and two rucksacks.

It was the end of this era of Taiwan history. The Japanese government would formally declare that its colonial authority had ceased on May 31, 1946. All remaining property and real estate of the Japanese were taken over by the KMT.

Summary Thought

The Japanese were the first to control the entire island of Taiwan. They had come with the idea to stay and their improvements were the most effective even though they treated Taiwan as a colony. During Japanese rule, the Taiwanese people had an unprecedented sense of participating in government; they along with the aborigines felt they were participating in something larger than the affairs of their group. How this would affect the future, remained to be seen.

Questions

What was Japan's vision of its sovereignty over Taiwan? Was Taiwan destined to be more than a colony?

What was the aborigines' changing perception of their position on Taiwan?

Did the Taiwanese feel that their destiny was still linked with the mainland after 50 years of Japanese rule?

Was there a difference in attitude between the educated Taiwanese and the working class Taiwanese?

What effect did the development of social organizations have on Taiwanese consciousness?

How did Taiwan's economy change with Japanese rule?

Additional Readings

Few works in English address this specific period by itself; rather it is
treated as part of a larger context. Numerous works by Edwin O.
Reischauer or Sir George Sansom can be chosen for this purpose.

Jones, F. C.. *Japan's New Order in East Asia*, Oxford Univ. Press,
1954, Oxford.

Takekoshi, Yosaburo. *Japanese Rule in Formosa*, trans. George
Braithwaite SMC Publishing Inc., 1996, Taipei. Written in 1907,
it explains the Japanese approach to Taiwan.

葉榮鐘等著，《台灣民族運動史》，台北，自立晚報社，1971。

周婉窈，《日治時代的台灣議會設置請願運動》，台北，自立報
系出版部，台北，1989。

黃昭堂，《台灣總督府》，東京，教育社，1981。

伊能嘉矩著、楊南郡譯，《台灣踏察日記》，台北，遠流出版
社，1996。

翁佳音，《台灣漢人武裝抗日史研究》，台灣大學文史叢刊74，
1986。

莊永明，《台灣醫療史》，台北，遠流出版社，1998。

楊碧川，《後藤新平傳》，台北，克寧出版社，1994。

矢內原忠雄著、周憲文譯，《日本帝國主義下之台灣》，台北，
海峽學術出版社，1999。

吳文星，《日據時期台灣師範教育之研究》，台灣師範大學史研
所專刊(8)，1983。

楊肇嘉，《楊肇嘉回憶錄》，台北，三民書局，1970。

若林正丈，《台灣抗日運動史研究》，東京，山本書店，1983。

淺田喬二，《日本帝國主義下の民族革命運動～台灣・朝鮮・滿州
における抗日農民運動の展開過程》，東京，未來社，
1978。

盧修一，《日據時代台灣共產黨史》，台北，自由時代出版社，
　　1989。
林鐘雄，《台灣經濟經驗一百年》，台北，三通圖書公司，
　　1995。
鄧相揚，《霧社事件》，台北，玉山社，1998。
陳銘城等編著，《台灣兵影像故事》，台北，前衛出版社，1997。
中村孝志編，《日本の南方關与と台灣》，奈良，天理教道友
　　社，1988。

IV

The Republic of China

From the Frying Pan into the Fire?

News of the Japanese surrender was broadcast by radio in Taiwan on August 15th 1945. On September 2nd, under order No. 1 from the Japanese General Headquarters (GHQ), the Japanese gave up their authority on Taiwan and the government of the Republic of China began preparations to take over. In October, an initial twelve thousand military personnel and two hundred officials landed on the island. At first, the people happily welcomed the Chinese military, but their joy soon turned to disappointment at the soldiers' lack of discipline and plundering attitude.

The soldiers coming off the boat were not an elite spit and polish group but remnants of an army that after struggling for victory over the past eight years was now embroiled in a continuing civil war. It was natural for the people to compare them with the well-disciplined Japanese soldiers that were leaving and wonder how they had won. Still the common people justified this disparity in their minds by saying that the Chinese must have had "superior kung-fu skills."

Chen Yi (陳儀), the ROC representative and first senior officer to govern the island, continued to carry out the Bao-jia system. He also made sure the chief positions in the government, the political party, the military authority and special mission organizations were given to people coming from mainland China. The incoming KMT was suspicious of anyone who had been under Japanese rule for fifty years and felt it was necessary to de-Japanese them. The people, however, felt that they had just traded one colonial government for another. Instead of being treated as liberated brothers, they were seen as the spoils of war.

As the civil war with the communists on the mainland continued, Taiwan suffered. Any and all materials and goods needed to support the KMT's efforts were taken from the island. Inflation became rampant; the economy came to a standstill. Most Formosans had difficulty finding work; unemployment skyrocketed. In matters of justice, those in authority were easily bribed. The living conditions of the people deteriorated.

Under Japanese rule, even during World War II, Taiwan was relatively unaffected. As a matter of fact, never in the people's 400-year history on Taiwan had they ever experienced a "shortage of rice." Now when they were supposedly "liberated," rice was scarce. The surprise and anger of the Formosans began to build.

The 2–28 Affair

Finally on February 27th 1947, a simple conflict between the police and a street vendor would touch off waves of protest across the island. The street vendor was selling contraband cigarettes that had been smuggled in; 6 policeman discovered this and confiscated the goods. When the woman asked for the return of the goods, one officer struck her with the butt of his gun. A crowd gathered to intercede for the woman, and the officer, feeling nervous, fired his gun. A stray bullet hit a bystander and killed him. The crowd grew angry.

On the following day, the 28th, a larger crowd came to the government offices asking for justice in this situation. The sentries fired on this unarmed crowd killing many and injuring more. In the mind of Chen Yi, the crowd was made up of thugs and the action was justified. In the minds of the people, they were simply seeking justice in an unfair situation. Protests immediately broke out all over the island. Two years of building anger at mistreatment by the Mainlanders exploded. Shops and factories were closed; students went on strike.

The popular anger would continue in forms of protest until the middle of May when the military might of the new government succeeded in quelling the outward protests. This protest and subsequent brutal suppression has been dubbed "er-er ba" or "2-28." Even today after 50 years, the date cannot be mentioned in Taiwan without drawing a strong emotional response depending on the background of the person to whom you are talking.

It is difficult to give an exact interpretation of the 2-28 affair since many of the historical records have been lost or destroyed. Likewise, people could not talk openly about it for over 40 years and now when the climate is more open, many of the survivors have already passed away. Some foreigners who witnessed the affair in person have recorded their experiences and made them public.

Allan J. Shackleton, a New Zealander, is one such person. He had been assigned as an engineer by the UN to help rebuild the broken industry of Taiwan in 1947. Upon returning to his country, he recorded his experiences of the 2-28 affair and called it *Formosa Calling*. This was published posthumously by his family in 1998. Another work, *Formosa Betrayed*, written by George H. Kerr, American vice-consul in Taiwan in 1947, was published in 1965. These two writings present the views of third party observers and accent the injustice and brutality of the time.

In Taiwan, as was said, it would be taboo to speak about this affair until after the lifting of martial law in 1987. At the time of the protests, Chen Yi gave orders to arrest anyone suspected of anti-government activities and many of the Formosan educated elite were seized in the name of social security. According to the published reports of the KMT government, almost 28,000 people would be killed; of these the majority were members of the intellectual class, creating a vacuum among the native Formosan intellectual elite.

Overseas Independence Movements

Some of the educated Formosans escaped from being arrested and fled overseas. In Hong Kong (then under British rule), a group of those with a strong identification and sympathy to Taiwanese consciousness, organized, under the direction of Riao Yuen-yi (廖文毅) the "Taiwan Re-Liberation Alliance." These concerned people petitioned the United Nations to express their wishes that Taiwan be put in trust before the UN would determine whether Taiwan should be allowed to vote on independence or not.

In Kyoto in 1950, Riao organized a political party, the "Taiwan Democratic Independence Party." After six years, his party attempted to establish a temporary government for a Republic of Taiwan in Tokyo. Later, in 1965, Riao would suddenly decide to surrender himself to the KMT, as the KMT held several of his relatives hostage to compel him to give up his independence activities.

Wang Yu-de (王育德) and his circle of the "Taiwan Youth Cooperation" in Tokyo organized a second Taiwan Independence movement. In the 1960's many Taiwanese students studying in the United States established other independence organizations and the center of Taiwan independence moved to America. In 1970, Taiwanese intellectuals living in Japan and the States jointly established an international "Taiwan Independence Alliance" and developed branches around the world.

The Republic of China on Taiwan

In the meantime, the civil war with the communists did not go well for the KMT. The Communist forces proved more adept at drawing the support of the common people. By August 1949, the Chinese Communists established their own regime and called it the People's Republic of China (PRC). At the end of the same year, Chiang Kai-shek and his army had escaped to Taiwan to continue their battle.

The KMT had lost most of the territory on the mainland and now occupied only Taiwan, the Pescadores and some smaller islands such as Kinmen (金門) and Matsu (馬祖). The population of Taiwan increased by some 2,000,000 people; it was the largest influx the island had ever seen. Inflation continued to run rampant.

Although the KMT had lost the mainland, the idea of retaking it would be preserved until 1991. In the meantime, the newcomers controlled the military and the political machinery; and the native Formosans faced a problem of unemployment.

By the end of 1949, after spending billions of dollars, the United States government was having its doubts about the KMT because of its corruption, and had ceased to support it. President Truman was willing to let the chips fall where they may and leave the PRC and ROC to work the matter out. If the Communist forces would attack Taiwan, the United States would stand aside. But again, happenings in Korea would affect the fate of Taiwan.

The Korean War and the Fate of the ROC

On January 5th, 1950, President Truman told reporters that the United States would not use its Armed Forces to interfere in the present situation between the PRC and the ROC and that "the United States Government will not pursue a course which will lead to involvement in the civil conflict in China." He had also purposely put nothing in his budget under the category of assistance to China. But on June 25th, 1950, North Korea with the aid of the Soviet Union invaded the South. The United States saw this as a larger communist threat to the free world and responded quickly by coming to the defense of South Korea.

This involvement would make the United States reverse its position on Taiwan. Now it was not salvaging a corrupt government but was preventing what was seen as the spread of global Communism. Truman now stated the following.

> "In these circumstances the occupation of Formosa by Communist forces would be a direct threat to the security of the Pacific area and to the United States forces performing their lawful and necessary functions in that area.

> Accordingly I have ordered the 7th Fleet to prevent any attack on Formosa. As a corrollary of this action I am calling upon the Chinese Government on Formosa to cease all air and sea operations against the mainland. The 7th Fleet will see that this is done. The determination of the future status of Formosa must await the restoration of security in the Pacific, a peace settlement with Japan, or consideration by the United Nations."

In January 1951, military aid was provided for the KMT. A joint defense and mutual aid agreement was signed and a military consultant and regiment was assigned to Taiwan. Most important of all, the United States Navy's 7th Fleet began patrolling the Taiwan Strait, thereby preventing any attack by the Chinese Communists. At the same time, the KMT realized it must root out its corruption.

In 1953, the Korean War would end in a stalemate at virtually the same place that it had begun for both sides, and the Cold War would ensue. Taiwan, however, had become part of the Western Bloc.

The Last Battle?

The Communists would make a concerted military effort in 1954 to capture Kinmen (Quemoy) and islands that lay only 2 kilometers off the coast of the Mainland. After several days of shelling, an attack was launched and landings made. Fierce fighting ensued for several days as both armies struggled for victory. The Communist forces would be defeated and numbers were taken prisoner. This marked the last battle between the two forces. The island of Kinmen would be shelled regularly for several years, but both sides would enter their own cold war. In December 1954 another joint defense treaty was concluded between the KMT and the government of the United States ensuring Taiwan's protection.

An Unresolved Status

While the ROC was now a member of the United Nations and

part of the strategy to stem communism, there was still an unresolved aspect of Taiwan's history. What was the exact relationship of Taiwan and the ROC? In the San Francisco Treaty of 1952, Japan had given up its sovereignty over Taiwan, the Pescadores and other territories; but the treaty did not state to whom the sovereignty of these areas would be given.* President Truman had at first been open to letting the PRC and the ROC settle this matter between them, but now with the Korean War and the belligerent threat of the PRC to stability in the region the matter was left in uncertainty. Even the ROC was not that directly interested in Taiwan; its focus was still on regaining mainland China.

* The Multilateral Treaty of Peace with Japan, September 8, 1951

The treaty was signed at San Francisco in 1951 by the respective Plenipotentiaries of the United States of America and 47 other Allied Powers, and Japan. It went into effect in 1952. In Chapter II on Territory, Article 2 reads:

(a) Japan, recognizing the independence of Korea, renounces all right, title and claim to Korea, including the islands of Quelpart, Port Hamilton and Dagelet.

(b) Japan renounces all right, title and claim to Formosa and the Pescadores.

(c) Japan renounces all right title and claim to the Kurile Islands. . . .

(f) Japan renounces all right, title and claim to the Spratly Islands and the Paracel Islands.

The Hand Writing on the Wall?

The sixties brought the Viet Nam Conflict and the issue of Taiwan's sovereignty was put on the back burner as the United States and other western nations feared the domino effect of communism in Asia. Taiwan continued to prove valuable as a place for surveillance of the PRC, for the R&R of US military personnel and for military supply linkage and strategy.

As the Viet Nam Conflict wound down another series of events happened that would affect Taiwan. The ROC's insistence on being the sole representative of all of China would eventually lead to the loss of its seat in the United Nations in 1971. Instead of sharing a seat with the PRC, the ROC chose to withdraw from the United Nations.

In 1972, President Nixon made his historic visit to mainland China. Then in December 1978, as more and more countries chose to recognize the PRC as the government of China, President Carter dropped his bombshell that the United States would shift its embassy from the ROC to the PRC in the coming year.

After the loss of the UN seat, thinking in the ROC began to change. There was the growing realization that the KMT's chances of retaking the mainland were growing slimmer and slimmer. Revenue that the KMT was storing up for the development of a retaken mainland was seen as being better spent on infrastructure development in Taiwan. From all the signs, the KMT was going to be on Taiwan for some time, so it had better make the best of it.

In 1975, Chiang Kai-shek (蔣介石) died and his son Chiang Ching-kuo (蔣經國) took over, first as the head of the KMT and then as President of the country in 1978.

Developments and Stories to be Written

There is much that has been written on Taiwan in the past fifty years, but the many unanswered questions indicate that there is much still to be written. The Taiwan Miracle has been well documented as Formosa, now formally called Taiwan changed its agrarian structure in the sixties, developed an export economy in the seventies and became one of the strongest economies in Asia and throughout the world for that matter.

The country began its move towards democracy in the last phase of Chiang Ching-kuo's presidency and has never looked back. Whether Chiang was far-sighted and visionary or whether he was bowing to inevitable realities seen in the protests over the Chung-Li Affair (中壢事件) in 1977 and the later Kaohsiung Incident of 1979 is a story still to be told.

The Kaohsiung incident, the first major human rights demonstration in Taiwan, and its orchestrated suppression by the KMT, would prove to be a watershed in the move to democracy on the island. The list of those jailed and brought to trial, along with their legal counsel reads like a "Who's Who" of the future Democratic Progressive Party (established 1986).

Chiang Ching-kuo is credited with recognizing and allowing opposition parties to develop, yet the reasons why a "White Terror" atmosphere existed in politics from 1947 all the way until 1987 when martial law was formally revoked have yet to be fully explained.

When Chiang Ching-kuo died, Lee Teng-hui, the hand-picked successor of Chiang Ching-kuo became President in 1988. He would be the first native-born Taiwanese to be president. The democratic process would continue under him. Lee would also declare an end to hostile relations between Taiwan and the Mainland in 1991. He would be re-elected in 1996 amidst the missile crisis with mainland China. This would be the first time the people could directly vote for their president. The extent and depth of Lee's contributions to the democratic process in Taiwan as well as other areas are also a story to be written. Lee's contributions to democracy will have to be balanced with his tolerance of "black gold" politics and corruption.

A Coming to Terms with the Past

The culmination of the democratic movement in the past years was the election of March 2000, when Taiwanese for the second time in their history voted directly to determine their president. It was a new millennium and a new era. Ousted at that time was the

KMT, which had held power in Taiwan for 55 years, but most outstanding was the fact that it was a true democratic election and the transference of power was peaceful.

Chen Shui-bian (陳水扁) of the Democratic Progressive Party (DPP) was elected with a plurality of 39.3%, second was James Soong (宋楚瑜), Independent with 36.84% and third was Lien Chan (連 戰) the KMT candidate with 23.10%. Two other candidates took the remaining 0.76%. It was a hotly contested race.

The PRC tried to influence the elections by hinting that Chen was the one candidate of the three that they did not want. It was a repeat of 1996 when the PRC fired missiles at both ends of the island to indicate that they did not want Lee Teng-hui elected. On both occasions they failed; the people made up their own minds. The candidate the PRC did not want was elected.

Chen had only won by 39.3% and not a full majority; but full majorities are not always had in a democracy. A quick glance at the history of the United States reveals many instances where the president won by less than 50% of the vote, and even cases where the losing candidate had a greater popular vote than the winner. Chen's victory percentage was slightly less than that Abraham Lincoln had received (39.82%) when he was elected in 1860.

The election marks another milestone in the history of Taiwan. It was a coming to terms with 400 years of history. It was a coming to terms between the KMT and the Taiwanese that all future choices in government would be made by the democratic process. If the KMT were to rule in the future, it would have to gain the majority support of the people. The people of Taiwan have been finally allowed to choose their destiny and not be the pawns of the power politics of history.

Unfinished Business

There still remains the unfinished business of the PRC. The PRC did not exist before the Cairo Conference or the Potsdam Conference* and the San Francisco Peace Treaty with Japan does not mention it. Yet the PRC, whose flag has never flown over Taiwan, insists that Taiwan has always been a part of China and that this issue is strictly an internal one. Should the 23 million people of Taiwan be forced to submit to the PRC? Should Taiwan be denied representation in the United Nations where 75% of the member countries have a population smaller than Taiwan? In the year 2000, the island nation of Tuvalu, with a total land area of 26 square km. and a population of only 9,000 was approved to become the 189th member of the United Nations. The reader is asked to examine the sovereignty issue and other issues in the light of the history of Taiwan and come to his/her own conclusions.

* The Potsdam Conference, July 26, 1945

Proclamation by the Heads of Governments, United States, China and the United Kingdom: "We the President of the United States, the President of the National Government of the Republic of China and the Prime Minister of Great Britain, representing the hundreds of millions of our countrymen, have conferred and agree that Japan shall be given an opportunity to end this war. . . . (8) The terms of the Cairo Declaration shall be carried out and Japanese sovereignty shall be limited to the islands of Honshu, Hokkaido, Kyushu, Shikoku and such minor islands as we determine."

One Year and Counting

The first anniversary of Chen Shui-bian's election shows a country still finding its way politically with its own share of crises. The Democratic Progressive Party has had difficulty adjusting to being the ruling party and coming up with a consistent ruling philosophy while the Kuomintang has found it difficult to adjust to the role of being the opposition party. In the Legislative Yuan, the KMT has repeatedly allied itself with New Party legislators and others to use their majority to only question the budget and to challenge and block legislation of the fresh president. This is despite the fact that many of these leaders had studied in the United States and had witnessed life in a democracy.

The People First Party has developed from the constituency supporting independent candidate James Soong. Because of this, in the coming elections for the Legislative Yuan in December 2001, no party is expected to receive a full majority and a coalition government will be necessary.

Chen's inability to solve the Legislative Yuan issue has made it difficult to deliver on many of his campaign promises most noticeably the halting of construction on the Fourth Nuclear Power Plant. The elimination of "black gold" political corruption has had limited success.

The fears expressed by many that Chen would declare independence and cause havoc in the Taiwan Strait have not materialized as Chen has repeatedly displayed an openness to discuss differences with the PRC. On the other hand his overtures have met with rejection until he first accepts the PRC's definition of "one China."

Small gains have been made with the establishment of three mini-links with mainland China through Kinmen and Matsu, Further, the President's good will visit to Central American allies, with an unprecedented extended stopover in the United States, has gained needed international recognition and exposure for Taiwan.

The greatest challenge facing the new administration, however, and one that most immediately affects the population, is how to rejuvenate the country's slumping economy. The stock market has continued to drop and Taiwan's unemployment rate has risen to approximately 3.8%. This may be a desirable percentage by the standards of most countries, but it is the highest in the current history of Taiwan. What lies ahead for this fledgling democracy? It is still too early to tell.

Summary Thought

Taiwan's most recent period presents the most controversy, perhaps because it is most close at hand. The Taiwan Miracle cannot be denied and credit must be given to the KMT as well as to the determination and entrepreneurial spirit of the people.

Taiwan has also become a full-fledged democracy. Beginning with the democratic movements from the "Danwai" (黨外) era in the 1950's and continuing on through the founding of the Democratic Progressive Party, democracy has not come easy, but it has come. This achievement is also a credit to the sacrifice and determination of the people not only on Taiwan but also to those overseas, both as students and in organizations particularly in Japan and in the United States of America. Yet despite Taiwan's democracy, the ambivalence of the major powers of the world continues to be seen in their treating Taiwan as an equal economically but not politically. And the aborigines, these people, once masters of the island, now play a marginal political role but they have full citizenship in Taiwan.

Questions

When the Allies gave Taiwan to the ROC were they giving it in trust? Could they return it to a party that did not exist in 1895?

Were the suppression of 2-28 and the subsequent "White Terror" necessary or were they used as a means to eliminate political opposition?

What is the PRC's claim to sovereignty over Taiwan?

Can the elections of 2000 be seen as a separation of the KMT from the ROC?

What should be made of the UN Charter's support of the right of people to choose their form of government?

Additional Readings

Gibert, Stephen P. and William M. Carpenter. *America and Island China*. University Press of America, 1989, Lanham, Maryland. Major documents and correspondence in the relations between the United States and the ROC, 1949–1988.

Kerr, George H. *Formosa Betrayed*. Houghton-Mifflin, 1965, Boston.

Shackleton, Allan J.著、宋伯亞譯，《福爾摩沙的呼喚(Formosa Calling)》，台北，望春風文化事業公司，1999。

Kerr, George H.著、陳榮成譯，《被出賣的台灣(Formosa Betrayed)》，前衛出版社，1997。

陳佳宏，《海外台獨運動史》，台北，前衛出版社，1997。

陳銘城，《海外台獨運動四十年》，台北，自立報系出版部，1992。

彭明敏·黃昭堂著、蔡秋雄譯，《台灣在國際法上的地位》，台北，玉山社，1995。

Cabell Phillips著、李宜培譯，《杜魯門總統任內錄》，香港九龍，今日世界出版社，1970。

林鐘雄，《台灣經濟發展四十年》，台北，自立晚報出版部，1987。

李筱峰，《台灣民主運動四十年》，台北，自立晚報出版部，1987。

Epilogue

Timor, another island, is north of Australia; it is about the same size as Taiwan but with a smaller population. The Portuguese settled the East Side of Timor around 1520. The Dutch settled the West Side one hundred years later and the island was split under the rule of these two countries. With the formation of Indonesia and the ousting of the Dutch, West Timor became a part of the Republic of Indonesia.

In 1975 when the Portuguese abandoned East Timor, it declared independence; but this independence was short-lived. Indonesia quickly invaded and took over East Timor. Unrest followed and finally Indonesia granted the people of East Timor the right to choose their destiny.

On August 30, 1999, 800,000 East Timorese voted over-whelmingly to be independent. Again violence ensued as West Timor militias refused to accept the vote. The United Nations, which had never approved the original takeover by Indonesia, stepped in and sent an international peacekeeping force to quell the violence. East Timor now is rebuilding its country.

The question naturally arises that if the United Nations would step in to protect the rights of 800,000 people in East Timor, would it protect the rights of the 23,000,000 people of Taiwan if force were used to settle the Taiwan question.

The world had seen a previous intercession by an international coalition when Iraq invaded Kuwait. Kuwait, a former British protectorate, had become independent in 1961. In 1990, Iraq invaded the country but was defeated in what is known as the Persian Gulf War. While one wonders if the intervention would have been as swift if Kuwait had not been an oil-rich country, the jury is still out on the Taiwan issue.

Island in the Stream
A Quick Case Study of Taiwan's Complex History

著　　者	April C. J. Lin & Jerome F. Keating
發 行 人	魏　德　文
發 行 所	南天書局有限公司
地　　址	台北市羅斯福路 3 段 283 巷 14 弄 14 號
	☎(02) 2362-0190　Fax:(02) 2362-3834
郵　　撥	01080538（南天書局帳戶）
網　　址	http://www.smcbook.com.tw
電子郵件	E-mail:weitw@smcbook.com.tw
國際書號	ISBN 957-638-576-8
版　　次	2000 年 10 月初版一刷
	2001 年 7 月二版一刷
印 刷 者	國順印刷有限公司

IV. 中華民國時代

　　1945年太平洋戰爭結束，伴隨日本的敗戰，日本被迫放棄以台灣、
澎湖爲始等所有其舊屬殖民地，台灣的歷史進入了「中華民國時代」。
在美國及其他列強的強勢主導下，台灣的命運被中華民國的國民政府從
接管到領有，至今亦超過了半個世紀。在這近半個世紀的歷程中，台灣
被捲入中國內部國共內戰的愛恨情仇、與冷戰時期國際社會美蘇兩大陣
營的對立局勢當中。另一方面，反觀島內伴隨時間的推移，政治上從威
權、解嚴、乃至政黨輪替的多重戲劇性轉變；經濟上從美援時代逐步走
向綠色矽島的理想；文化上從中華文化復興運動重新回歸至社區總體營
造、提升本土意識的問題思考方向；社會上從安定、繁榮的終極指標轉
向志工台灣、福利國家的社會集體價值之追求，這一切在在展現出台灣
民眾在國內外艱困的政治環境中雖然背負著「雨夜花」的命運，卻一直
抱持永不放棄希望的「望春風」精神。

　　2000年3月18日台灣民眾以直接民選的方式選出了第一位非國民黨
籍的總統，台灣的民主工程又開始了一個新的里程碑。在新的執政黨與
總統帶領下，台灣必需重新思考自己未來的定位與走向，從國家認同與
文化省思的問題思考開始；與中國之間兩岸關係能否持續穩定發展；以
及其所衍生而來的外交困境之突破、族群與意識形態對立態勢的消弭；
透過島內社會黑金、特權的掃除以期能開創公平競爭的社會環境；以及
如何減輕新世紀台灣產業升級等問題所帶來的經濟遲緩成長與失業率攀
升的衝擊。爲了能成爲國際社會的正式成員，以及維護亞太地區的繁榮
與安定，即使前途險惡，但台灣民眾一如過去仍努力地站在世界的激流
中屹立不搖。

謹識於2001年6月21日

ISLAND IN THE STREAM
A Quick Case Study of
Taiwan's Complex History

著　　者: April C. J. Lin & Jerome F. Keating
出 版 者: 南天書局有限公司
出版日期: 2000年10月初版
　　　　　 2001年6月再版　　　淡江大學歷史系副教授　林呈蓉

從台灣的國際定位談起

　　姑且不論國內統獨意識如何地壁壘分明，每年到了秋天聯合國會議期間、或是四年一次的美國總統大選時，從兩岸議題所衍生出來台灣的國際定位問題，經常成爲眾人爭議的焦點。經過海內外媒體不斷地炒作之後，即使原本不關心政治、歷史的一般群眾，特別是外國人士、或是華僑第二代、第三代子弟，也開始注意起這樣的「國際性」話題。他們的第一個疑問多半是「台灣怎麼會讓自己走進這條死胡同裡呢？」

　　在聯合國裡面，有近百分之七十五的會員國人口是少於台灣的。位於歐洲的列支敦斯登(Liechtenstein)人口僅有3萬2千左右；更甚者如太平洋上的獨立島國Tuvalu成立於1978年10月，在1995年當時人口也僅有1萬左右，但是在聯合國內他們也有投票權；反觀坐擁2千3百萬人口的台灣卻失去了在聯合國的席次，進而坐失了投票權。問題是聯合國內這些小國寡民之會員國的一票也可能左右台灣2千3百萬民眾的生存權。

即使台灣的經濟實力在世界排名第15（1999年），世界多數的國家也都願意視台灣為一獨立個體，而與之進行經貿、文化交流；但是礙於中國的阻撓，台灣在國際社會的政治、外交地位卻無法被大多數的國家所認同。在無視於台灣民眾情緒的情況下，中國仍舊片面地宣稱「台灣自古就是中國的一部份」。

是台灣人抑或是中國人

翻開中國歷代疆域變遷圖來看，似乎很難證明台灣「自古」便歸屬於中國。四百年來島上的政權更迭不斷，從荷蘭人政權時代開始、歷經了東寧王國政權、清廷政權、日本人政權、國民政府政權等不同政權的時代。在民族意識與國家認同的議題上，所謂「上有政策、下有對策」，政權頻繁更易的歷史脈絡下，島上的民眾逐漸磨練出一種能夠隨時彈性因應的能力。然而，台灣人民目前所面臨前所未有最大的難題是，連「一天」都未曾統治過台灣的「中華人民共和國」政權，也宣稱其對台灣具有主權性。

姑且不論「國共紛爭」給台灣帶來如何的影響，單從民眾史的觀點重新審視這個議題，不禁令人質疑「國家」這種人為的體制，有時似乎不能給民眾帶來福祉，反而是把一般百姓的生活步調給攪亂了。從清國人、日本國皇民、到中華民國國民，在這個島上有不少人一生中已經經歷了三個不同政權的時代。從台灣短短四百年的時間進程中五度易幟的歷史脈絡裡，便可推知，即使世界其他地方應該也存有類似的問題，但皆不如台灣的案例如此別具代表性。

III. 日本帝國時代

　　1895年清、日之間由於甲午戰爭因而簽訂了馬關條約，根據條約內文之規定，清帝國同意把台灣、澎湖割讓給日本。從此台灣的歷史進程跨入了「日本帝國時代」。日本帝國時代在台灣的歷史發展上佔據了五十年的時間，卻給日後的台灣社會帶來極其深遠的影響，而「近代化」則是其中一項最爲具體的時代特質，也爲戰後的五〇、六〇年代台灣的經濟發展多所助益。在日本統治期間，從上下水道工程建設等衛生環境的整備開始；推動人口、戶籍、舊慣、土地、林野等各項基礎調查事業；並統一幣制以促進金融與商業的流通；建設與擴充各種交通運輸事業；開發水力與火力發電廠以奠定日後台灣發展工業的動力基礎；並從品種改良開始重振台灣傳統重要的米糖經濟產業。

　　台灣的近代化經驗幾乎是在與日本的近代化同步的情況下發展起來，但無可諱言地，日本帝國在台灣所奠定的一連串近代化基礎，基本上完全是爲了配合帝國內部資本主義發展的需求所設計的，然而如果台灣史上欠缺了這一段歷史經緯，把今天的台灣社會與中國治下的海南島相比，則恐怕也無出其右。

　　值得一提的是，伴隨此一時期日本在台灣辦理了近代的國家教育，也導致1915年之後台灣的民變不同於以往，乃逐漸具備了近代民族運動、社會運動的特質。台灣民衆在自立救助的過程中，一反過去的草莽行徑，不斷展現出試圖在現行體制內爭取自身權益的決心。一種蘊含近代國家特質的社會運動，從1920年開始直至1937年因中日戰爭的爆發而必須終止一切的組織活動爲止，乃成爲台灣社會抵抗外來政權統治的一種新潮流。

帝國的版圖裡，但是在清帝國對台灣212年的統治當中，前面的190年期間對台灣的經營管理，則採行消極方針的統治政策。配合清帝國外交上的閉關自守策，台灣被迫暫時退出了國際舞台；另一方面，在清帝國強勢的大陸政權統治下，台灣一直站在整個帝國結構的末端與邊陲位置上。直至幾個事件發生之後，才逐漸改變了台灣這種被迫自閉的命運：一爲1858年清帝國與列強訂定四國天津條約，決定台灣開港（淡水、雞籠、安平、打狗），乃促使台灣有機會再次重回國際舞台；1874年日本對南部台灣出兵，引發了牡丹社事件，促使清帝國在台灣的經營管理上，一改過去的消極路線，進而轉換成積極的統治方針，獎勵大陸內地民眾移民台灣；1885年清法之間原是爲了越南問題而引發清法戰爭，但竟有一個戰場是位在毫無瓜葛的北台灣（雞籠、淡水），由此顯見西方列強對台灣別具野心，也促使清帝國重新思考台灣的行政定位，於是台灣在戰後正式獨立建省，脫離了過去附屬在福建省下的命運。

在清帝國統治時代中，「民亂頻仍」成爲極其矚目的一個時代特色。然而，這種「三年一小反、五年一大亂」的現象基本上乃是傳統中國社會所存在的一種社會特質，伴隨著大陸民眾「唐山過台灣」的移民過程，又把這樣的社會特質移植到了台灣社會，進而塑造出台灣「民亂頻仍」的形象。台灣的民亂除了一般的抗官民變之外，還包括民間透過族群、姓氏、職業團體的勢力結合所導致的分類械鬥。這種民變頻仍的社會現象，充分顯示出台灣社會長久以來一直都是處在一種不安定的狀態當中，而構成其不安定的根源主要有三：第一、社會公權力在許多時候經常無法有效伸張，因此民眾總是必需設法自立救助；第二、多數時候台灣社會都是被外來政權所統治，且政權更迭頻仍，經常無法滿足在地住民的真實需求；第三、不同族群一起寄居在如此蕞爾小島上，族群相互之間經常必需面對激烈的生存競爭。

內容導覽

雖然歷史學家難以爲這樣的史實馬上做出論斷，但是以台灣歷史爲題材，從歷史學、政治學、與社會學等各種分野角度，討論國家認同與民族意識等問題時，應該能從民眾史的立場上推衍出一些可深入探討的課題。因此，即使在《Island in the Stream》書中對每一段歷史脈絡並沒有特別的預設立場，但是在各個章節最後皆提示幾個可供共同討論的議題，並且提供幾本可以深入探究的專書，以資讀者參考。

全書一共分爲四個章節：根據台灣四百年來的發展歷程，分爲：I. 大航海時代、II. 清帝國時代、III. 日本帝國時代、IV. 中華民國時代。

I. 大航海時代

在「大航海時代」中，我們提供讀者一個「無主地(open territory)」的概念，台灣這個島嶼原來不屬於任何勢力所有。島上居民的主要成員爲原住民，以及少數來島上貿易、傳教、兼營局部開墾事業的外來者。原住民的組成結構分歧複雜，若以其分布的地理位置而論，則大致可分爲高山、平埔等兩大系統。屬於平埔系統的原住民多半都與漢人通婚、同化，如今已被混入大多數「台灣人」的血脈裡。高山系統的原住民則由於活動空間較爲偏僻，因此現今從中央山脈往東行走，仍隨處可見到他們的蹤跡。島內的外來者則包括了鄰近的日本人、伴隨新航路・新大陸發現而來的荷蘭人、西班牙人、以及橫行東亞海域富可敵國的鄭氏海上武裝貿易集團等。台灣所扮演的「亞太營運中心」角色，在這一時期表現得淋漓盡致。

II. 清帝國時代

時期逐漸往後推移至「清帝國時代」，雖然朝廷決定要把台灣納入